PORSCHE

The Legend

PORSCHE
The Legend

Jonathan Wood

Page 1: The Porsche badge, which features the arms of the city of Stuttgart where the company is based, set against those of the state of Baden-Württemberg. The horse on the city's arms indicates that it was founded on the site of a stud farm. The badge, created in response to Porsche customers overseas, appeared on the 356's steering wheel boss from 1953 and the bonnets of the cars in 1954. Page 2: The distinctive Porsche rear profile shown to advantage on a 1990 Carrera 4. Page 3: New for 1997, the acclaimed open two-seater, mid-engined Boxster will take Porsche into the 21st Century.

Figures and data in this book are quoted in metric measurements first, with the Imperial equivalents noted in brackets.

This is a Parragon book
This edition published in 2004

Copyright © Parragon 1997

Parragon
Queen Street House
4 Queen Street
Bath BA1 1HE, UK

Designed, produced and packaged by
Stonecastle Graphics Ltd

Edited by Philip de Ste. Croix

ISBN: 1-40544-336-7

Printed in Indonesia

Photographic credits:

All photographs by **Neill Bruce Motoring Photolibrary**, with the exception of the following: *(Abbreviations: r = right, l = left, t = top, b = below)*

Porsche Cars GB and the Peter Roberts Collection c/o Neill Bruce: 3, 6, 7(*t*), 7(*b*), 10, 11(*t*), 18, 35(*t*), 36, 37(*t*), 38-39(*b*), 42, 43(*b*), 44, 45(*b*), 46, 47(*l*), 48-49, 49(*t*), 51(*b*), 55(*t*), 56, 57(*b*), 58, 68, 69(*t*), 69(*b*), 70, 72(*l*), 74, 76, 77, 78, 79(*t*), 79(*b*).

Bay View Books Ltd: 8, 17(*l*), 21(*t*), 21(*b*), 23(*t*), 33(*b*), 43(*t*), 50.

David Hodges: 24, 38(*l*), 39(*t*), 49(*b*).

Andrew Morland: 29(*t*), 29(*b*), 45(*t*).

Fred Hampton: 14.

Neill Bruce and the publishers would like to thank all the owners who have made their cars available for photography, especially the following:

Mike Barker at The Midland Motor Museum: 356 Carrera 2 (page 15); 911 RSR (page 30-31); 924 record car (pages 34-35) and 911 Carrera Speedster (pages 66/67).

Nigel Dawes: 928 (pages 40-41) and 928 S4 (page 59).

Duncan Hamilton Ltd: 917K (pages 26-27).

Dick Lovett Ltd: 959s (pages 60-63).

The Earl of March for the wonderful Goodwood Festival of Speed.

Special thanks to Ms Fiona Loader of Porsche Cars Great Britain, for arranging cars for photography and helping with archive material.

Contents

Introduction

TO MISQUOTE a popular song, there is nothing like a Porsche*. From the company's birth in 1948, the theme has been an unorthodox one of producing a distinctive sports car with aerodynamically refined bodywork and powered by a rear-mounted, horizontally opposed, air-cooled engine.

Sometimes this German firm has strayed into more orthodox pastures, and the results have invariably been fine cars, although they have somehow lacked spirit and persona.

Porsche has now reverted to what it does best, which is encapsulated in the current 911, a design that, incredibly, first appeared back in 1963.

Porsche cars are as they are because the first model, the 356, was inspired by the Volkswagen, created by the Stuttgart-based design bureau that Ferdinand Porsche had established in 1931. In addition to manufacturing cars, the company still sells its engineering expertise to the world's motor industry.

When the great Austrian engineer's son, also christened Ferdinand but always known as Ferry (born 1909), decided, in mid 1947, to produce a sports car under the Porsche name, it was both logical and inevitable that its mechanicals would be based on those of the VW.

This meant its cost-conscious, rear-mounted, air-cooled, 1.1 litre, four-cylinder engine. Its horizontally opposed configuration is known on the Continent as a boxer motor.

Porsche-patented torsion bar suspension was similarly employed and, whilst the VW parts progressively made way for Porsche-designed ones, the theme was perpetuated on the 911 which replaced the 356 in 1964. Here was one of the great designs of motoring history and it is, in essence, still in production today.

Porsche was fortunate to be buttressed by royalty payments from booming VW Beetle sales, but in 1975 came what proved to be an ill-advised corporate switch in emphasis away from sports cars, and towards more popular grand tourers powered by conventional front-mounted, water-cooled engines.

In the short term the arrival of the 924, followed by the 928 and 944, saw an astonishing rise in sales volumes, which peaked in 1985/6 when 53,625 cars were produced.

However, from thereon output has slumped to a 13,000-unit, 18 year low in 1993 as the GTs have ceased production, and the 911 sports car has again moved centre stage.

Left: Ferry Porsche (right) with the first Gmünd-built 356 aluminium coupé. Completed in June 1948, it was bought by enthusiast R. von Senger of Zurich.

6

* Pronounced Por-sha

Note: The Porsche model year begins in August of the previous calendar year i.e., a 1996 model year car appears first in August 1995.

Left: Ferry Porsche's pre-production Beetle cabriolet in the early post-war years at Gmünd, the company's premises in the Austrian Alps.

Below: The VW-based Porsche Type 64 of 1939 marked the first stirrings of the make, and is seen at Porsche's Stuttgart home. Only three were made. The prototype Volkswagens were built in the garage behind.

Almost from its inception the company has participated in racing. The first Porsche appeared at Le Mans in 1951 although it was to be 19 years before the make took the chequered flag in the 24 hour classic event in 1970.

Since then Porsche has won on a further 11 occasions, and these 12 victories are now unrivalled by any other make. Ferrari's long reign of nine triumphs at the Sarthe circuit is vanquished.

Currently Porsche is still a proudly independent company as its grapples to survive in an increasingly competitive world. As its half century as a major manufacturer approaches in 1998, the extraordinary chemistry of Germany's most famous sports car still excites enthusiasm, awe and, above all, respect.

Porsche 356

THE NO frills 356 of 1948 was the first Porsche and its unconventional appearance and rear-mounted, air-cooled engine established a unique pedigree that endures until this day.

Called 356 because of its allocation in the company's register of designs, the cars were initially built at a former saw mill in the Austrian Alps because Porsche's Stuttgart premises were occupied by the American army. The bureau had occupied the remote facility at Gmünd since 1943 so as to be out of range of Allied bombing.

An open car, its mechanicals were laid out under Ferry Porsche's direction by chief engineer Karl Rabe, and based on the Type 64 sports coupé Porsche had built before the war. As the company had been responsible for the design of the Volkswagen Beetle saloon, this 1939 car was powered by its horizontally opposed, four-cylinder, air-cooled engine that, in the interests of roadholding, was located in the centre of the vehicle. The layout was inherited by the 356.

However, at the elder Porsche's suggestion, on production versions the 1.1 unit was relocated in the rear position it shared with the VW saloon to provide, albeit limited, accommodation for rear passengers. As on the Volkswagen, the Porsche-patented torsion bar suspension was all independent, with trailing arms at the front and a rear swing axle.

Whilst this prototype had an open body, essayed by Erwin Komenda, the majority of 356s were aerodynamically superior aluminium coupés. As such they were capable of a respectable 136km/h (85mph).

Production, such as it was, continued at Gmünd until 1951. But in the previous year Porsche had returned to Stuttgart, although not to its original factory. Instead it shared facilities with the Reutter body company, with which it had strong pre-war associations, and it was not until late in 1955 that the firm reoccupied its own premises in the Zuffenhausen district of the city.

Reutter was accordingly awarded the 356 body contract and the shells were now made of cheaper but heavier steel. To compensate for the extra weight, in 1951 the 356's engine capacity was upped to 1.5 litres. Later, for the 356A of 1956, came a final increase to 1.6.

In 1950 the first 356s had appeared in America, which was to become Porsche's most important overseas market. British sales started in the following year.

The company made its Le Mans debut in 1951 when a trio of 356s were entered. Although two dropped out, the third went on to win its class. This was an impressive showing for what was essentially a standard car. Clearly the new Porsche marque was one to watch!

Left: A Gmünd-built, German-registered 356 coupé. The divided windscreen featured until 1952.

SPECIFICATION	PORSCHE 356
ENGINE	Flat 4, 1100cc
HORSEPOWER	40bhp @ 4200rpm
TRANSMISSION	Manual 4-speed
CHASSIS	Platform
SUSPENSION	Independent front and rear
BRAKES	Hydraulic drum
TOP SPEED	136km/h (85mph)
ACCELERATION	0-96km/h (60mph): 17.6 seconds

Left: A 356A cabriolet in action. Below: A 1951 356
coupé as owned by British Porsche enthusiast Betty Haig.

9

Porsche 550 Spyder

THE 550 of 1953 was Porsche's first purpose-designed sports racer and, as such, is the ancestor of a long and distinguished line that has been developed in tandem with the road cars.

In the early 1950s, there was only one Porsche model, the 356, so the 550 was inevitably closely related to it. Its starting point was a 356-based spyder (open) car, created in 1950 by VW dealer, Walter Glockler of Frankfurt.

Built on a light tubular frame with an open body and powered by a tuned 1.1 engine, Glockler enjoyed some success in sports racing with the car, which he repeated in a second 1500cc special in 1952.

It was this car that represented the starting point of the factory-built 550 which appeared in 1953 and which was also 1500cc-powered. Two examples ran at Le Mans in coupé form when they dead heated in the 1500cc class and paved the way for the definitive 550 that arrived in 1954.

This was distinguished by a purpose-designed, roller-bearing engine, the work of Dr Ernst Fuhrmann, and whilst the 1.5 litre unit retained the four-cylinder, air-cooled theme of the 356, its pushrods were replaced by shafts and a train of raucous gears to activate high efficiency twin overhead camshafts. Developing 110bhp, this was more than double the output of the road car unit.

Like the prototype 356, it was positioned in the middle of the car; overhauls of this complex four were reputed to take some 200 hours!

The 550 Spyder was completed in time for the 1954 season and Mille Miglia race, where one won its class and was sixth overall. At Le Mans came triumphs in the 1500 and 1100cc classes, the latter being suitable for a small-bored version of the design.

The model was also available for public sale and eventually about 100 were built, with the majority crossing the Atlantic to America. The factory was again successful at Le Mans in 1955 where they repeated the class wins of the previous year.

Below: The mid-engined 1954 Type 550 Spyder that ran in gruelling Carrera Panamericana races.

In 1956 the design was revised as the lighter 550A which had a space frame and modified rear suspension, whilst engine power was upped to 130bhp. A five-speed gearbox was employed.

A 550A, driven by Umberto Maglioli, in 1956 gave Porsche its first victory in the Sicilian Targa Florio road race, an event that it was to dominate with a total of 11 successes.

The purposeful, potent and, above all, reliable 550 family of silver roadsters was responsible for establishing Porsche as a serious competitor in sports-car racing. Even so the make's full potential had yet to be realized.

Above: A 1956 550A with lighter and stiffer space frame chassis. Right: A later 550A of 1959 vintage.

SPECIFICATION	PORSCHE 550 SPYDER
ENGINE	Flat 4, 1498cc
HORSEPOWER	110bhp @ 7800rpm
TRANSMISSION	Manual 4-speed
CHASSIS	Tubular ladder type
SUSPENSION	Independent front and rear
BRAKES	Hydraulic drum
TOP SPEED	201km/h (125mph)
ACCELERATION	0-96km/h (60mph): 7.8 seconds

Porsche 356 Speedster

BY THE early 1950s, it had become clear that America had emerged as Porsche's most important overseas market. Therefore in 1954 it introduced a model that, initially, could only be bought by trans-Atlantic customers.

An open body, known in Germany as a cabriolet, had been a feature of the 356 since the model's outset and, in 1952, the company had introduced a shadowy, US-destined, open two-seater 356 named the American Roadster. This, in turn, paved the way for the 356 Speedster.

It was the New York-based Max Hoffman, Porsche's US importer since 1950, who suggested to the factory that it produce a stripped, lower cost, open version of the 356 to compete with the likes of the British Austin Healey 100 and Triumph TR2.

The outcome was the two-seater Speedster, a combination of the cabriolet and American Roadster. It differed from the mainstream open car by its wrap-around windscreen, and the door waistline was reduced by 35mm (1.4in). The hood was distinctively lower and shorter than the norm and, when lowered, folded completely out of sight.

Below: A 1955 356 Speedster as owned by Betty Haig.

SPECIFICATION	PORSCHE 356A SPEEDSTER
ENGINE	Flat 4, 1582cc
HORSEPOWER	72bhp @ 4500rpm
TRANSMISSION	Manual 4-speed
CHASSIS	Platform
SUSPENSION	Independent front and rear
BRAKES	Hydraulic drum
TOP SPEED	153km/h (95mph)
ACCELERATION	0-96km/h (60mph): 13.5 seconds

The flat, as opposed to curved, instrument panel was also peculiar to the model and was dominated by a speedometer and revolution counter; the upper part of the dashboard was upholstered.

Right: Rear view of the 1955 Speedster 1500. Below: The unique instrumentation of a 1600 Speedster.

Seating was also a departure from previous practice with the fitment of sporty lightweight bucket seats. Power came from a 55bhp, 1500cc engine, although the 70bhp 1500S was available at extra cost.

At $2995 the Speedster was the cheapest Porsche to be sold on the American market but this price was only possible because the revolution counter and heater were specified as options!

It was more accelerative than the heavier but more aerodynamically efficient 356 coupé, although its top speed of 152km/h (95mph) was marginally less.

Nevertheless, the Speedster soon became popular in American sports-car racing and in sunny California. The model established a modest but loyal following that has elevated it to cult status over the years.

When the much improved 356A series appeared for 1956, the Speedster was accordingly updated with a new top line 1600 engine.

The model was due to be revised for the 1959 model year and this new, better-equipped version, built by Drautz of Heilbronn rather than Reutter, was instead titled the Convertible D, a name which perpetuated an American designation.

So after four seasons the Speedster was discontinued, but this open 356 remains as the most memorable, if not handsome, of these early Porsches.

13

Porsche 356 Carrera

IN 1955 the Carrera name joined the Porsche model range; it has been a formidable part of it ever since. Initially it was applied to the most potent road car of the day, the first example of which appeared, along with the 356A family, at that year's Frankfurt Motor Show.

The model was so named in recognition of Porsche's victories in the Carrera Panamericana Mexico races between 1952 and 1954. Outwardly it closely resembled the standard 356 models but the real differences were beneath the rear engine cover!

The 1.5 litre power unit was essentially a detuned version of the potent but noisy twin-overhead-camshaft, roller-bearing engine which had already appeared in the 550 Spyder sports racer of 1954.

Dr Fuhrmann, the power unit's designer, had fitted one in his own coupé and the concept received a rigorous baptism when a 356, equipped with this competition-honed engine, won the demanding Liège-Rome-Liège Rally in 1954.

Officially designated the 356-1500 GS,

Porsche's original intention was to build 100 cars so that it could qualify for participation in the grand touring class. In addition to its fitment in the coupé, the engine was also available in the Cabriolet and Speedster.

In road form, it generated 100bhp in place of the racer's 110 although, similarly, dry sump lubrication was employed. The model's top speed of a magic 200km/h (124mph) made it the fastest 1.5 litre road car of its day.

Inside the Carrera had a wood-rimmed steering wheel and the instruments were changed to reflect the more powerful engine. The rev counter now ran to 8000rpm and the speedometer to 250km/h (155mph). Bucket seats were fitted.

SPECIFICATION	PORSCHE 356 CARRERA
ENGINE	Flat 4, 1498cc
HORSEPOWER	100bhp @ 6200rpm
TRANSMISSION	Manual 4-speed
CHASSIS	Platform
SUSPENSION	Independent front and rear
BRAKES	Hydraulic drum
TOP SPEED	200km/h (124mph)
ACCELERATION	0-96km/h (60mph): 11.3 seconds

Left: A 1956 356 Carrera 1500GS. Above: 1964 Carrera 2. Right: A 1960 Abarth Carrera GTS with Zagato body. A 2 litre Abarth-tuned engine was employed and only a few were built.

For 1958 the capacity of the engine was increased to 1.6 litres and it differed from the original in being fitted with conventional plain bearings, in place of the noisier built-up Hirth roller crankshaft.

In 1962 came the 2 litre Carrera 2 which was the first Porsche road car to be fitted with disc brakes. It was relatively successful in races and rallies and built in limited numbers until 1965. But by this time the factory's purpose-designed sports racers had taken over from the 356-bodied car.

The Carrera name had, however, become an established one. It was briefly revived on Porsche's sports-racing 906 Carrera Six of 1967 although it would not be until 1972 that it was applied to a potent version of the 356's 911 replacement.

Porsche 356B & C

THE final manifestation of Porsche's formative sports car line, the 356C, introduced for the 1964 season, had a relatively brief life and overlapped with its fabled 911 successor by a year.

Outwardly the 356C was similar to its 356B predecessor. This had appeared for 1960 and was outwardly similar to the A. but the discerning enthusiast recognized a larger rear window than previously and the engine cover now possessed two cooling grilles instead of one. The C was similar but the hub caps were flat topped which indicated the presence of all-round disc brakes.

The C's 1.6 litre engine was essentially that of the 356B; the standard model developed 75bhp whilst the 1600S produced a further 20bhp. The two-seater roadster, a feature of the 356 range since 1954, was discontinued on the C, so leaving three body styles. There was the familiar coupé whilst the omnipresent Cabriolet could be specified in relatively rare hardtop form, as well as in its popular hooded guise. For the first time this possessed a detachable rear window.

The C was, arguably, the best of the 356 family; performance was essentially the same as its B Series predecessor, as it possessed a top speed of

Right: The only way to tell the difference between a 356C and its B predecessor is the flat-topped hub caps indicating the presence of all-round disc brakes. Below: A very presentable example of a 1.6 litre 356C engine, still clearly Volkswagen-based but with an increasing number of Porsche parts.

SPECIFICATION	PORSCHE 356C
ENGINE	Flat 4, 1582cc
HORSEPOWER	75bhp @ 5200rpm
TRANSMISSION	Manual 4-speed
CHASSIS	Platform
SUSPENSION	Independent front and rear
BRAKES	Hydraulic disc
TOP SPEED	175km/h (109mph)
ACCELERATION	0-96km/h (60mph):12.2 seconds

Left: Classic lines, a 356B, which featured an enlarged rear window, in an historic car race in Sweden.

some 175km/h (109mph). This was coupled with the customary Porsche reliability.

However, in the autumn of 1964, production of the new six-cylinder 911 began, initially at the rate of five cars a day, which compared with some 40 examples of the 356C.

But as 911 totals began to rise, so the C's started to fall and, in April 1965, the last example, a flower bedecked white Cabriolet, left the Zuffenhausen production line.

As the first Porsche model, the 356 had been responsible for introducing this new German marque to the world of motoring. A total of 76,303 examples had been built since 1948, of which 16,668 were 356Cs.

But this was not, after 17 years of production, quite the end of the story. For in 1965 came the 912 which featured the new 911's body powered by what was, in essence, the 356C's 1.6 four-cylinder engine.

The 912 was built until 1969, but even then the 356 influence proved enduring because the concept was revived after a six-year interval in 1975. This followed the world rise in oil prices when this export-only model was marketed as the 912E, for economy. Only when the last one was built in 1976 was the lineage of this first Porsche model finally laid to rest!

Porsche 904 GTS

THE FINAL sports racing expression of the Porsche four-cylinder line came in 1964 with the arrival of the 904 GTS coupé. It not only took the first two places in that year's Targa Florio event but was also second in the 1965 Monte Carlo Rally and scored a host of class wins, in addition to numerous other competition successes.

The 904's appearance coincided with the arrival of Porsche's new 911 road car. Its six-cylinder engine was developed by technical director Hans Tomala, who had replaced Karl Rabe in 1962. He was also responsible for the design of the new mid-engined coupé. It differed from previous Porsches by having glass-fibre bodywork made, incidentally, by the Heinkel aircraft company. This was bonded to a box-section, ladder-type chassis which resulted in a extremely rigid structure.

Whilst there were thoughts about fitting the 904 from the outset with the 911's six-cylinder engine, because this was an unproven unit it was decided instead to employ the potent and reliable 2 litre Carrera four.

Porsche's intention was to build 100 such cars for homologation. A similar number would be produced for the 1965 season with the new six in place of the ageing four.

In the event the 1965 series was never implemented; a total of 120 cars were built, of which 104 were fours and 10 used the freshly minted six. The remaining six cars were powered by a 2 litre flat eight unit developed for Porsche's 804 Formula 1 racing car of 1962.

The 904 immediately proved its worth with the 1964 Targa Florio victory, where its lively

Below: The glass-fibre-bodied 904GTS of 1964. Most were powered by the Carrera's four-cylinder engine.

18

qualities and reliability on the twisting circuit trounced the mostly Italian opposition. At that year's Le Mans all five of the coupés survived, with the first car home coming in seventh.

But in 1965 Hans Tomala departed and that year Ferry Porsche's nephew, Ferdinand Piech, took over as head of the experimental department. He had little interest in the 904 although it was maintained as a stop-gap model, powered by sixes and eights, until the arrival of its 906 successor in 1966.

This was not before a six-cylinder 904 had achieved fourth place at Le Mans in 1965, behind a trio of Ferraris, where it ran faultlessly throughout the 24 hours. Its engine employed a magnesium crankcase, which in 1969 replaced the aluminium one on the 911, an example, if one was needed, of racing undoubtedly improving the breed.

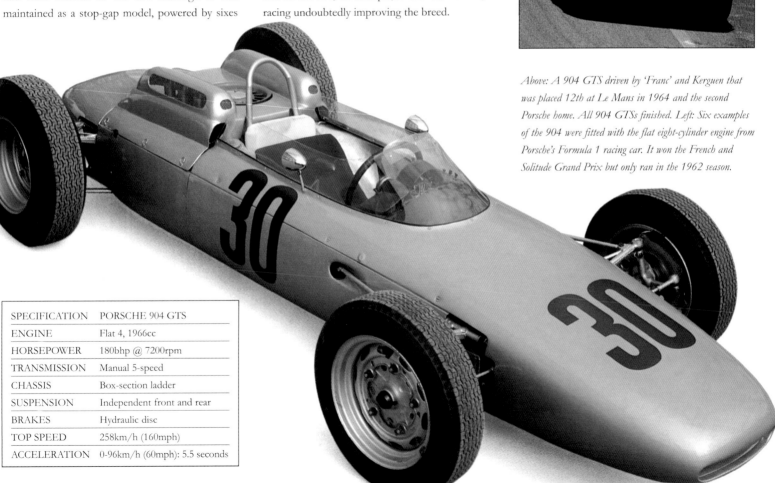

Above: A 904 GTS driven by 'Franc' and Kerguen that was placed 12th at Le Mans in 1964 and the second Porsche home. All 904 GTSs finished. Left: Six examples of the 904 were fitted with the flat eight-cylinder engine from Porsche's Formula 1 racing car. It won the French and Solitude Grand Prix but only ran in the 1962 season.

19

SPECIFICATION	PORSCHE 904 GTS
ENGINE	Flat 4, 1966cc
HORSEPOWER	180bhp @ 7200rpm
TRANSMISSION	Manual 5-speed
CHASSIS	Box-section ladder
SUSPENSION	Independent front and rear
BRAKES	Hydraulic disc
TOP SPEED	258km/h (160mph)
ACCELERATION	0-96km/h (60mph): 5.5 seconds

Porsche 911 & 911S

THERE CAN be no question that the most famous numerals in the Porsche lexicon are 911. This was the name allotted to an all-new model which, in 1964, extended the rear-engined, air-cooled line begun with the 356. Such has been success of the concept that today, 33 years on, it is still in production.

The car, launched at the 1963 Frankfurt Motor Show and the product of a four year gestation, was a sleek coupé with its contours uncluttered by fripperies and, as such, the design has proved to be remarkably enduring. These memorable lines were essayed by Ferry Porsche's eldest son, Butzi, and skilfully refined by Erwin Komenda. In addition, the 911 was some 100mm (4in) longer than the 356 that made it a more practical two plus two seater. It was also faster.

Like the body, the 911's 2 litre engine was completely new, although the horizontally opposed, air-cooled configuration, established on the 356, was perpetuated.

But there the similarities ended, because this was a 2 litre six, not a four and, in place of the Volkswagen-inherited pushrods, were chain-driven single overhead camshafts per cylinder bank. Thereupon rockers activated high efficiency inclined valves. Dry sump lubrication was employed.

Although Porsche-patented torsion bars remained as the suspension medium, they were used at the front in conjunction with MacPherson struts, and at the rear with semi-trailing arms.

Ironically this most famous Porsche model number began life on its introduction as the 901. But the French Peugeot company, which had used a central 0 as a model designation since the 1920s, objected and Porsche responded by replacing the digit with a 1.

In 1966, just two years after the 911 entered production, Porsche introduced a more potent version of the model which it called the 911S.

This was instantly identifiable by the fitment of handsome Fuchs five-spoke forged alloy wheels.

In its standard form the 2 litre engine developed 130bhp, but the S unit produced 160, the result of it being fitted with stronger forged – as opposed to cast – pistons, new camshafts, larger valves with better porting and a 9:8 rather than 9:1 compression ratio.

In consequence the 911S's top speed of 220km/h (137mph) was some 16km/h (10mph) faster than the already potent basic model.

Roadholding was also improved on all the 1969 cars when their wheelbases were extended by 57mm (2.24in). For 1970 engine capacity was increased to 2.2 litres, and then to 2.4 in the 1972 model year. Although the 911 had initially used carburettors, with the arrival of the 1974 range all cars employed fuel-injected engines. These were to be the first of many modifications because this was a model that was to run and run . . .

Left: 1967 911S with identifying alloy wheels. Above right: A 2 litre 911 of 1965 and the fifth right-hand-drive car to reach Britain. Right: A 911 interior of 1965/66 with wood-rimmed steering wheel. The instruments included an oil level indicator for the dry sump system.

SPECIFICATION	PORSCHE 911
ENGINE	Flat 6, 1991cc
HORSEPOWER	130bhp @ 6100rpm
TRANSMISSION	Manual 5-speed
CHASSIS	Unitary
SUSPENSION	Independent front and rear
BRAKES	Hydraulic disc
TOP SPEED	209km/h (130mph)
ACCELERATION	0-96km/h (60mph): 8.3 seconds

Porsche 911 Targa

AN OPEN body had been part of the Porsche line since 1948 but when the 911 arrived it was only available in coupé form for the first two years of its manufacturing life.

This deficiency was rectified on the 1967 models with the appearance of a particularly ingenious convertible version named the Targa, in honour of Porsche victories in the Sicilian Targa Florio road race.

The 356C Cabriolet had ceased production in 1965, but when they came to develop an open version of the 911, Porsche engineers were constrained by what they believed would be an aspect of impending US safety regulation.

As America was the company's most important single market, it could ignore this legislation only at its peril. This was interpreted, incorrectly as it transpired, as the compulsory fitment of a safety

roll-over bar to protect occupants of a convertible in the event of an accident. One was therefore incorporated.

In addition, the Stuttgart team grappled with a problem that had become apparent on the 356. As the speed of the model increased, it became progressively more tiring to drive the open version with its hood raised, on account of wind noise and

Below: The definitive Targa with fixed rear window and roof panel in place. The roll-over bar is ingeniously concealed by the stainless steel hoop. This is a 1973 car with optional alloy wheels.

SPECIFICATION	PORSCHE 911 TARGA
ENGINE	Flat 6, 2341cc
HORSEPOWER	165bhp @ 5600rpm
TRANSMISSION	Manual 5-speed
CHASSIS	Unitary
SUSPENSION	Independent front and rear
BRAKES	Hydraulic disc
TOP SPEED	225km/h (140mph)
ACCELERATION	0–96km/h (60mph): 6.9 seconds

buffeting. Germany's autobahns that were designed for sustained high speed motoring emphasized this deficiency.

The outcome was the Targa, which Porsche described as the 'world's first safety convertible', that was unveiled at the 1965 Frankfurt Motor Show, although it did not enter production until late in 1966.

It made ingenious use of a safety roll-over bar which spanned the rear of the car behind the front seats and was concealed with a broad strip of satin-finished stainless steel.

The roof was available in two alternative forms. There was a removable plastic section or a collapsible hood, both of which could be stowed in the front luggage compartment.

Behind the bar was a section of hood zipped into place rather like that used on the 356 Cabriolet. As it transpired the solution was not wholly satisfactory because, in practice, the rear window perpetuated the noise problem and it also leaked.

Therefore the 1969-model-year 911s saw the arrival of the definitive Targa top with the detachable roof panel standardized and the rear section replaced by a fixed rear window of moulded glass. It made the car less of a convertible, but proved an admirable solution being both water-tight and snug in winter.

As a result the Targa became very popular. By 1967 it accounted for no less of 40 per cent of 911s built and remained in production for close on 30 years, only eventually being updated in 1995.

Right: Targa in its original form with the canvas rear window folded down. Below: A 912 Targa competing in the 1970 Monte Carlo Rally.

Porsche 917

SPECIFICATION	PORSCHE 917
ENGINE	Flat 12, 4494cc
HORSEPOWER	520bhp @ 8000rpm
TRANSMISSION	Manual 4- or 5-speed
CHASSIS	Aluminium space frame
SUSPENSION	Independent front and rear
BRAKES	Hydraulic disc
TOP SPEED	348km/h (216mph)
ACCELERATION	N/A

PORSCHE had participated in the Le Mans 24 hour race since 1951. Although it had achieved numerous class wins and attained a second placing in 1968, outright victory had proved elusive.

The company therefore decided on the construction of a purpose-designed car to meet new regulations for a 3 litre prototype or 5 litre 'production' sports car of which at least 25 had been constructed. Porsche chose the latter option and the result was Ferdinand Piech's 917, that was one of the most powerful racing cars of its day.

Porsche unleashed the massive 4.5 litre 917 at the 1969 Geneva Motor Show and its presence was tantamount to a declaration, if one had been needed, of the company's bid for the Le Mans prize.

It had already produced a flat eight engine for its Formula 1 car of 1962 which was followed by an enlarged 3 litre unit for the 908 sports racer of 1968.

For the 917, Porsche went one stage further and added a further four cylinders to produce a flat 12 of 4.5 litres capacity that was, in effect, two 911 engines mounted in tandem. It was, of course, air cooled and thus dominated by a large plastic-bladed cooling fan. This formidable 3ft-long (914mm) power unit developed an eyebrow-raising 520bhp.

Mid-located in a multi-tubular aluminium chassis, the mechanicals were cloaked in a glass-fibre body which could be fitted with a choice of tails. An elongated one was intended for the 24 hour event.

A pair of works 917s and a privateer entered the race. Both factory cars retired whilst in the lead

and the third crashed killing its driver. But this was not before one of the trio was timed at 319.2km/h (198.4mph) down the Mulsanne Straight.

When the 917s returned in the 1970 event, their bodywork was modified with revised front ends and swept-up tails. Mechanically some 917s were fitted with 5 litre engines, so bringing them to the maximum size permitted by the regulations.

But it was a 4.5 litre car, entered by Porsche Salzburg and driven by Hans Herrmann and Richard Attwood, that gave Porsche its richly deserved first Le Mans triumph. Another 917 was in second place.

It was the same story in 1971 when these mighty cars, by now developing over 600bhp, once again came in first and second.

They also triumphed across the Atlantic in the Can-Am series of 1972 with the revised 917/10K

(the latter letter referred to *kompressor*, indicating the fitment of twin turbochargers). This endowed the flat 12 with 900bhp and proved invincible. It also dominated the 1973 races, by which time the 917/30 was developing an astounding 1100bhp and had a theoretical top speed of 418km/h (260mph)!

Below: Porsche's first victory at Le Mans was achieved with the 917 driven by Herrmann and Attwood. Right: The model in ultimate twin-turbocharged 917/30 guise and one of the Roger Penske 1973 team Can-Am cars.

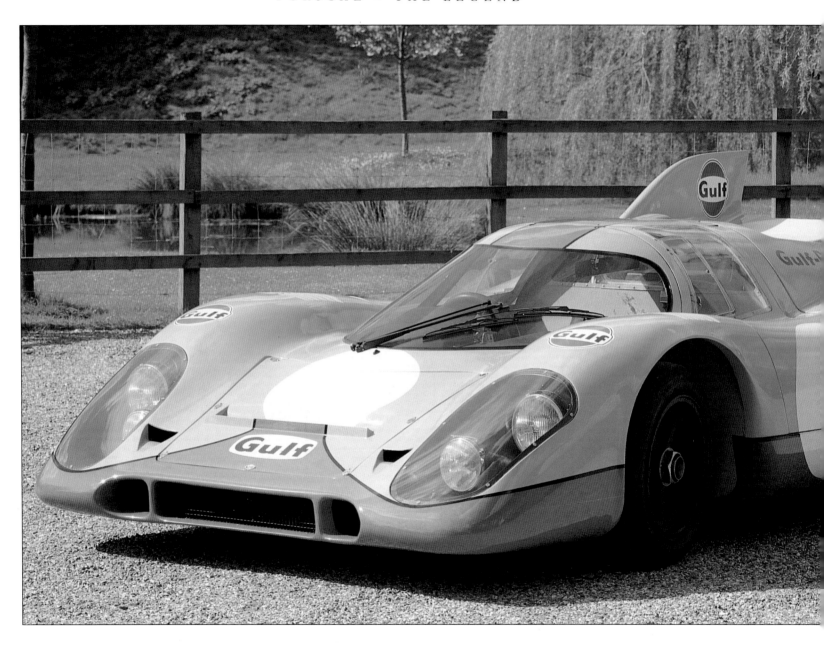

Left: In its original 1969 form the 917 suffered from disastrous handling, a shortcoming that was largely rectified by changes to its bodywork. The 917K – for kurz (short) tailed car – was better behaved than the longer one. This 917K is the 1969 car that Piper and Gardner drove in that year's 1000km Nürburgring race, where they were placed eighth. It is seen here in Gulf Oil livery with body modifications as introduced for the 1971 season. Left: The driving compartment. Below: Head-on view of the 917K run by John Wyer's J.W. Automotive racing team.

27

VW-Porsche 914/6

UP UNTIL 1969 Porsche had only produced rear-engined road cars. But in that year the company introduced the 914 that was the first Porsche passenger model to have a mid-located power unit.

The product of the Stuttgart firm's close association with Volkswagen, Porsche was not, of course, a stranger to the mid-engined configuration. Its virtues of better balance, and thus handling, and the presence of a more compact power unit had already been applied to the sports racers.

On the debit side (for road cars) was a lack of interior space, more noise and difficulty of access, none of which had been constraints on competition machines.

The car came about because, in the mid 1960s, Porsche was beginning to think of developing a no-frills model in the 1950s spirit of the 356 Speedster. It was an approach that chimed with Volkswagen, still mass producing the Beetle but wanting to give a fillip to its utilitarian image. This had been achieved, to some extent, by its Karmann-built Karmann

Ghia sporty coupé, sales of which, however, had latterly been flagging.

Porsche agreed to design the car to accommodate Volkswagen's new 1.7 litre flat-four, air-cooled engine developed for its 411 saloon of 1968. However, the all-independent suspension was in the 911 idiom.

It was also conceived to be powered by the 2 litre 911 unit, as Porsche agreed to buy back bodies from Karmann in Osnabruck. They were then completed on the 911 production line.

Below: A British registered 1974 VW-Porsche 914/4, the Volkswagen version of the design. The panel from the Targa roof has been removed.

SPECIFICATION	VW-PORSCHE 914/6
ENGINE	Flat 6, 1991cc
HORSEPOWER	110bhp @ 5800rpm
TRANSMISSION	Manual 5-speed
CHASSIS	Unitary
SUSPENSION	Independent front and rear
BRAKES	Hydraulic disc
TOP SPEED	193km/h (120mph)
ACCELERATION	0-96km/h (60mph): 8.8 seconds

The outcome of this tripartite dialogue was, in retrospect, a rather curious-looking vehicle with push me/pull you lines that came from Gugelot Design near Stuttgart. These had been conceived for a front-engined car that was refined by Porsche for the mid location. It was consequently a genuine two-seater with a detachable roof panel in the Targa manner.

Below: 914/6, the Porsche version, instantly identifiable by its wheels and 914-6 badge on the rear. This is a 1970 car. The six-cylinder 911 engine was employed.

Above: Front of the German-registered 914/6 – there were no right-hand-drive cars. Luggage compartments feature both at the front and rear.

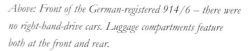

At the 1969 Frankfurt Show, the Porsche-powered 914/6 version was announced simultaneously with the VW-engined 914/4; it was faster and better equipped than its stablemate.

Whilst the latter was capable of some 177km/h (110mph), the Porsche was a 193km/h (120mph) car but it sold in relatively small numbers. Just 3333 were produced which compared with 65,351 VWs, many of which were sold in America where they were marketed under the Porsche name.

By 1975 both models had ceased production but, as will emerge, the close association between Porsche and Volkswagen was destined to produce some more surprises.

29

Porsche 911 Carrera

THE RESPECTED Carrera name reappeared on the Porsche road car range, after a seven year absence, for the 1973 season. Like its predecessor, this 911 was the most potent model in the line but, unlike the 356 version, it did not employ a purpose-designed engine.

It was, however, likewise ultimately intended for sports racing. Designated 911RS by the factory, the Carrera was based on a much lightened 911S body.

Although its 911 stablemates used a 2.3 litre engine, the Carrera was fitted with a big-bored, high revving 2.7 litre unit, that developed 210bhp, which compared with 165bhp of the 2.3 six.

In the interests of weight-saving, a glass-fibre engine cover was also used. It incorporated the now familiar 'duck's back' rear spoiler and was the first Porsche to be so equipped. Another first for a production model was the fact that the road wheels were wider at the rear than the front.

The Carrera was designed to compete in Group 4 GT competition which required that a minimum of 500 be built but, in the event, some 1600 were produced during 1973.

This was because it could also double as a road car in Europe, although this was not the case in America because it lacked emissions equipment, a state of affairs that was rectified in 1974.

Right: A 1974 Porsche 911 Carrera RSR, a customer racer, with 3 litre engine and spoilers front and rear.

These Carreras for street use accounted for about 600 of the total and featured the better appointed 911S interior. But the balance of 1000 or so were pukka sports racers.

This 2.8 litre RSR derivative soon established itself as a formidable performer. In America a privately entered example won the 1973 Daytona 24 and Sebring 12 hour races and a factory car also triumphed in that year's last Targa Florio race.

But from there on, as sports racing became more specialized, Porsche began developing purpose-designed although still 911-based cars, and the Carrera's role became that of a still potent but increasingly civilized road model.

The 911 range had soon incorporated the Carrera 2.7 litre engine for 1974 when the RSR went

30

SPECIFICATION	PORSCHE 911 CARRERA
ENGINE	Flat 6, 2687cc
HORSEPOWER	210bhp @ 6300rpm
TRANSMISSION	Manual 5-speed
CHASSIS	Unitary
SUSPENSION	Independent front and rear
BRAKES	Hydraulic disc
TOP SPEED	238km/h (148mph)
ACCELERATION	0-96km/h (60mph): 5.6 seconds

31

Above: A 1973 lightweight RS Carrera of thinner sheet metal than usual, no rear seats, glass-fibre engine cover and enlarged 2.7 litre power unit. Note that this example has no less than six front lamps!

to a full 3 litres. This, in turn, spawned the sports-racing turbocharged Turbo-Carrera in 1974, although its capacity was restricted to 2.1 litres.

As far as the 3 litre unit was concerned, this was extended to the 1976 Carrera road cars and the rest of the 911 family for 1978.

By this time the 911's evolution was stagnating as the new front-engined Porsches moved centre stage. The Carrera name was dropped from the 1978 season and remained in abeyance until the 1984 models, when it made a welcome and impressive return.

Porsche 911 Turbo

TAKING the Carrera RSR and its Turbo derivative as its starting point, in 1974 Porsche created the 911 Turbo road car, and this fabled model has been in production, almost without interruption, ever since.

A turbocharged passenger car was not new. In 1962 General Motors had pioneered the concept on its glass-fibre-bodied Chevrolet Corvette and, in 1973, BMW introduced the 2002 Turbo, which was Europe's first turbocharged production car. But it only remained in production until 1974 and a mere 1600 were built.

For Porsche the incentive was Group 4 homologation for its projected 935 sports racer, which required that a minimum of 400 road cars be constructed.

The company was, of course, no stranger to the turbocharger. It had featured on its 917 racer of 1972 and the 1974 Turbo-Carrera but, as a Group 5 participant, it had been restricted to 2.1 litres capacity. A road model had no such constraints so a turbocharged car, designated project 930 and based on the engine of the race-bred 3 litre RSR Carrera, was created relatively easily.

Below: The Porsche Turbo of 1975 with distinctive flared wheel arches and rear spoiler. Britain's Porsche concessionaires was AFN Ltd., and this was its demonstration car.

SPECIFICATION	PORSCHE 911 TURBO
ENGINE	Flat 6, 2993cc
HORSEPOWER	260bhp @ 5500rpm
TRANSMISSION	Manual 4-speed
CHASSIS	Unitary
SUSPENSION	Independent front and rear
BRAKES	Hydraulic disc
TOP SPEED	246km/h (153mph)
ACCELERATION	0-96km/h (60mph): 6.4 seconds

Having said that, the prototype exhibited at the 1974 Paris Motor Show was a non-runner, its turbocharger tract being a wooden mock-up! The car did not enter production until April 1975, a good six months later.

The finished product looked wickedly purposeful and was easily identifiable by its wider wheels with accompanying flared arches and the obligatory and identifying rear 'tea-tray' spoiler, which was usually what most other drivers saw as a Turbo swept past them.

Under the engine cover were the essentials of the 3 litre RSR unit and the KKK turbocharger was mounted on the left-hand side of the engine. In view of the extra power, 260bhp rather than the 200 of the 3 litre Carrera, a new gearbox was created for the Turbo, although with four rather than five gears.

Inside, it was the best appointed model in the 911 range, being fitted with air conditioning as standard, electrically operated windows and leather upholstery.

But it was the model's shattering performance that made the Turbo such a formidable car. Top speed was an impressive 246km/h (153mph) with

Above: The Turbo's 'tea-tray' rear spoiler living up to its name! Right: The Turbo's 3 litre engine with air conditioning pump on the right.

161km/h (100mph) coming up in just 14 seconds. Other bonuses were astonishing flexibility and petrol consumption of 14 litres/100km (20mpg).

The Turbo remained available in this 3 litre form until the 1978 model year when the engine was enlarged to 3.3 litres. As will emerge, that was far from the end of the Turbo story . . .

33

Porsche 924

UP UNTIL 1975 every Porsche road car was powered by a rear-located, air-cooled engine. But in that year came the first of a trio of models that featured conventional, water-cooled units. Not only that, the 924 was a Porsche for Everyman.

This was a car that, ironically, had begun life as a Volkswagen, a company with which Porsche had strong ties. Work on the project had begun in 1972 and its engine and running gear came from within the VW combine.

Porsche was already developing its own front engine/rear drive 928 model that, perversely, appeared after the 924. The VW project reflected its mechanicals with an in-line engine that drove a propeller shaft enclosed within a tubular backbone. This was balanced by a rear transaxle that featured a combined Audi gearbox and differential. The coupé hatchback body with aerodynamically friendly concealed headlamps was styled by Porsche's Harm Lagaay.

The 924's engine came from in-house Audi, the 2 litre fuel-injected unit having begun life in its 100 saloon. But it had been enlarged and converted to a more efficient belt-driven single overhead camshaft for use in the Volkswagen LT van range.

The MacPherson strut independent front suspension was courtesy of the Super Beetle whilst the rear semi-trailing arms also originated with the Beetle.

But by the time that the car was completed, Volkswagen was wrestling with the first deficit in its history and the fact that sales of the ageing Beetle were faltering.

So Porsche bought its own design back for

Below: In 1979 this AFN-entered 924 established a new British 2000-kilometre record at Snetterton circuit by averaging 122km/h (76mph) for 24 hours.

SPECIFICATION	PORSCHE 924
ENGINE	Straight 4, 1984cc
HORSEPOWER	125bhp @ 5800rpm
TRANSMISSION	Manual 5-speed
CHASSIS	Unitary
SUSPENSION	Independent front and rear
BRAKES	Front, hydraulic disc; rear, drum
TOP SPEED	201km/h (125mph)
ACCELERATION	0-96km/h (60mph): 9.9 seconds

Right: The final version of the model was the 924S and this Le Mans version dates from 1988, the final year of production. Below: Rear view of the AFN 924 that covered 704 laps of Snetterton circuit, a distance of 3033km (1885 miles).

DM 100 million (£16.2 million). VW made this conditional on the 924 being built by Audi at its Neckarsulm factory about 40km (25 miles) from Stuttgart.

Announced late in 1975, the 924 proved to be an instant success and became the best-selling Porsche of its day. Costing £7350 in Britain, which was some £3000 less than a 911, it brought Porsche ownership to a sector of the community that would never have previously contemplated one. The 50,000th example was built in 1979 and it only took a further two years for this 201km/h (125mph) car to reach the 100,000 mark.

In an effort to counter criticisms of harshness at high speeds, the 924 was re-engined for 1986 with a 2.5 litre four derived from its 944 stablemate. The redesignated 924S was now a 209km/h (130mph) car and it survived until 1988.

Porsche 935

PORSCHE was the first winner, in 1976, of the newly instigated World Championship of Makes and did it with the 911-Turbo-related sports-racing 935 that performed with remarkable consistency to repeat this triumph over the next three seasons.

This competition was intended to outlaw the so called '3 litre prototypes', in reality thinly disguised grand prix racers, that had hitherto dominated the World Sports Car Championship. They would be replaced by cars that maintained the visual outline of a production model and also retained its engine block.

Otherwise manufacturers could modify cars as they wished and that, of course, included turbocharging or supercharging the engine.

As far as Porsche was concerned, the 935's starting point was the Turbo-Carrera of 1974 and the enlarged 2.8 litre flat six now developed no less than 590bhp making the car capable of speeds in excess of 322km/h (200mph).

When the 1976 season started, the 935 which, as required by the regulations, outwardly resembled the 911 Turbo, proved its ascendancy by winning the first two races of the season. However, in the subsequent three events it was successfully challenged by BMW. Detailed modifications improved reliability and 935s took the first two places in the six-hour race at Watkins Glen, USA in July. It went on to win the final race at Dijon and with it the championship.

Nineteen seventy seven was even more successful with the now twin-turbocharged 935s returning a stupendous 630bhp. As such, they dominated the series by achieving first and second places in every round.

An interesting variation on the theme was the 935/78 of 1978, which was fitted with such an elongated body in the familiar Martini racing colours of white, blue and red, that it was popularly known as 'Moby Dick'.

Below: The sensational 911-based 935 of 1976.

SPECIFICATION	PORSCHE 935
ENGINE	Turbocharged flat 6, 2850cc
HORSEPOWER	590bhp @ 7500rpm
TRANSMISSION	Manual 4-speed
CHASSIS	Unitary
SUSPENSION	Independent front and rear
BRAKES	Hydraulic disc
TOP SPEED	336km/h (209mph)
ACCELERATION	N/A

*Right: A 935 of 1977 named 'Baby'
and so called because its engine capacity
was reduced to 1.4 litres and then
turbocharged. Driven by Ickx, it won
at Hockenheim. Below: The elongated
935/78, otherwise known as 'Moby
Dick', being driven by Derek Bell at
the 1996 Goodwood Festival of Speed.*

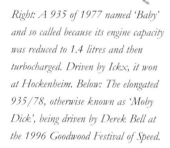

Its engine had water-cooled cylinder heads which permitted the use of four, as opposed to the usual two valves per cylinder, although otherwise air cooling was retained. This 3.2 litre turbocharged six developed 750bhp.

Moby Dick won its Silverstone debut but a potential victory at Le Mans in 1978 was never realized, the car coming in eighth because of persistent misfiring. But the 935's time would come in 1979.

In that year, ironically, the 935's sister car, the 936, did not repeat its 1977 victory but privately entered 935s took first, second and third places, so giving the company a well-deserved fifth victory at the Sarthe circuit.

Porsche 936

THE 936 sports racer, designed for Group 6 competition, gave Porsche its third Le Mans victory in 1976 and proceeded to repeat the feat in 1977 and 1981.

Unlike its 935 contemporary, the 936 of 1976 did not resemble the 911. Its chassis was related to the 908 racer of 1968 vintage, although the 2.1 litre turbocharged flat six engine was derived from that of the Turbo-Carrera. Outwardly the 936 bore a family resemblance to the mighty 917/30 of 1973, despite Porsche's claim that the design was new . . .

Two cars were entered for the 1976 Le Mans event but one withdrew with a fractured gearbox input shaft, which was the only 936 retirement of the season.

However, the Porsche driven by Jacky Ickx, amongst others, was briefly delayed on the Sunday afternoon by a broken exhaust pipe which neutered the turbocharger. But it went on to win the race, coming in 11 laps ahead of a French Mirage.

In the following year Porsche entered two 936s, now with twin-turbocharged engines. This time Ickx retired early but switched to the other 936 whilst it was in fifteenth place.

During the night he drove an inspired race and, by the following day, had worked his way up to second position, although was still some distance behind the leading Renault. This subsequently pulled out with a broken piston, so letting Ickx into the lead.

Below left: The Porsche 936/77, driven by Gregg and Haywood at Le Mans in 1978 where it was placed third.
Right: The winning 936/81, driven by Ickx and Bell, at Le Mans in 1981. It led the race from start to finish and covered 4825km (2998 miles) at an average speed of 201km/h (125mph).

SPECIFICATION	PORSCHE 936
ENGINE	Turbocharged flat 6, 2142cc
HORSEPOWER	520bhp @ 8000rpm
TRANSMISSION	Manual 5-speed
CHASSIS	Aluminium space frame
SUSPENSION	Independent front and rear
BRAKES	Hydraulic disc
TOP SPEED	322km/h (200mph)
ACCELERATION	N/A

Then, 45 minutes from the finishing line, the Porsche suffered a similar fate, but driver Hurley Haywood immediately went into the pits where the sparking plug was removed, his team mate Jurgen Barth then rejoined the fray and he went on to win on five pistons.

For this consecutive Porsche triumph, Jacky Ickx, the team and two 936s were accorded a civic reception on their return to Stuttgart.

At Le Mans in 1979, the three 936s dropped out but, as already mentioned, the marque scored a victory when a 935 took the chequered flag.

In 1980 the versatile 936 came in second, and a glorious swansong followed in 1981. Two much modified 2.6 litre 936s were entered and, whilst one car was plagued with reliability problems, Ickx and Derek Bell drove a copybook race in the other to win. This brought the number of Porsche's victories in the 24 hour event to six and Jacky Ickx became the most successful driver in the history of the event, having driven the winning car on no less than five occasions.

Left: The 1981 Le Mans-winning 936/81.

39

Porsche 928

FLAGSHIP of a corporate bid to move Porsche up-market, the 928 of 1977 was a costly front-engined, V8-powered grand tourer that bore no relationship to any previous model, although the 924 shared the layout of its mechanical components.

The 928 was the product of a restructured company as, in 1971, Ferry Porsche decided that what was essentially a family business had become inefficient through filial in-fighting. Its members were encouraged to find new positions outside the firm and a new chief executive, Dr Ernst Fuhrmann, appointed.

He is best remembered for the design of the 356 Carrera engine of the 1950s and came to Porsche from the Goertz piston company. Fuhrmann believed that the company's future lay in conventionally engined grand tourers, so the long running 911 was downgraded.

Left: A large hatchback was a notable feature of the 928. This is a 1979 car. Above: The 4.6 litre engine of a 1984 928S. An alloy V8 with single overhead camshafts per bank, it developed 300bhp.

The car that Fuhrmann ultimately regarded as its successor was the 928. But history has had the last word, because it is the 928 that is now obsolete and the 911 family is taking Porsche into the 21st century.

As it happened the 928 was unveiled to great acclaim at the 1977 Geneva Motor Show and it was voted Car of the Year in 1978.

With the emphasis firmly placed on weight saving, the Anatole Lapine-styled hatchback body featured aluminium doors, bonnet and front wings, while there were, apparently, no bumpers. In truth they were concealed beneath the nose and tail sections made of a plastic material that matched the body style. Ingeniously, these panels bounced back into shape after an impact.

SPECIFICATION	PORSCHE 928
ENGINE	V8, 4474cc
HORSEPOWER	234bhp @ 5500rpm
TRANSMISSION	Manual 5-speed
CHASSIS	Unitary
SUSPENSION	Independent front and rear
BRAKES	Hydraulic disc
TOP SPEED	225km/h (140mph)
ACCELERATION	0-96km/h (60mph): 6.8 seconds

Aluminium also featured in the 4.5 litre engine, that was Porsche's first V8, and incorporated single overhead camshafts per cylinder bank. Power was conveyed to a five-speed, differential-mounted gearbox via a flexible drive shaft that ran, in the 924 manner, within a tubular backbone. There was also the option of three-speed automatic transmission.

On paper here was the ultimate grand tourer, comfortable, sure footed and capable of 225km/h (140mph). Yet for all its ingenuity, opinions began

Above: Porsche moves up-market, a 928 of 1979.

to be voiced that this big car lacked the traditional vitality of a Porsche that was so exemplified by the 911.

These criticisms were heeded by the company, and in 1979 came the 928S that was powered by an enlarged 4.6 litre engine. As a result top speed went to beyond the 233km/h (145mph) mark, yet somehow the magic was still missing . . .

Porsche 911 Turbo 3.3 litres

FOR THE 1978 season the 911 Turbo's engine was enlarged to 3.3 litres and, for the first time, in addition to the familiar coupé it could be had in Targa and Cabriolet guises, although these variations did not arrive until 1987.

The fitment of this larger unit made the Turbo the largest capacity model in the 911 range as the engines of the mainstream cars were simultaneously increased to 3 litres.

The rise to 3.3 litres was created by enlarging both the bore and stroke, and it made the model even faster than the original. It was endowed with a top speed of 257km/h (160mph) and 161km/h (100mph) came up in just 12 seconds. This made the Turbo the fastest accelerating road car of its day.

The turbocharger was now fitted with an intercooler that had long proved its worth in racing. This device has the effect of reducing the temperature of the charged air and thus the efficiency of the boost.

On the Turbo it was located on top of the engine and was served by an enlarged rear spoiler that incorporated an air intake to serve it and the air conditioning radiator.

This necessitated the fitment of a full-width unit with raised rubber surround that instantly identifies the 3.3 from its predecessor. Otherwise the wider wheels and arches, together with the luxurious interior were perpetuated.

Less apparent was the fact that Porsche took the opportunity to uprate the braking system and servo assistance became a standard fitment.

Otherwise the volatile mixture that was the Turbo endured. This superb high performance car was perhaps most in its element on European motorways where it came into its own as the ultimate grand tourer, very fast, consistent and still relatively economical.

If the model had a limitation, it was that it still possessed a four-speed gearbox, as introduced in 1974. The original 911 five-speeder had been incapable of coping with the power generated by the 260bhp turbocharged flat six.

Left: A 3.3 litre Turbo of 1977, outwardly similar to its 3 litre predecessor but with identifying full-width rear spoiler. A standard 911 is in the background.

42

However, the 1989 season saw the arrival of a new, across-range, five-speed 'box that was also suitable for the Turbo. But soon afterwards, in mid-1989, the model was dropped from the Porsche line.

It did not remain unavailable for long and made a surprise reappearance at the 1990 Geneva Motor Show incorporating the Carrera 2's revised body blended with the established Turbo features.

Thus enhanced this 1991 car continued to be built until 1993 when the 911 body received its most radical revision since its appearance 30 years before.

Right: The Turbo's well equipped interior with leather seats, air conditioning and electric windows. This is a 1986 US specification car with revised switches and air vents.
Below: A slant nose conversion by the factory's Customer Department of a 1986 Turbo.

43

SPECIFICATION	PORSCHE TURBO 911 3.3
ENGINE	Turbocharged flat 6, 3299cc
HORSEPOWER	300bhp @ 5500rpm
TRANSMISSION	Manual 4-speed
CHASSIS	Unitary
SUSPENSION	Independent front and rear
BRAKES	Hydraulic disc
TOP SPEED	257km/h (160mph)
ACCELERATION	0-96km/h (60mph): 5.1 seconds

Porsche 924 Turbo

IF ANY real criticism could be levelled at the 924, it was its lack of Porsche-like acceleration. However, this shortcoming was remedied to a great extent by the arrival, in 1978, of the 924 Turbo.

It was discovered that the 924's 2 litre engine was more than capable of coping with the stresses of turbocharging, but a new cylinder head was required with inlet valves able to sustain the higher temperatures generated. The exhausts were also enlarged.

These modifications, coupled with the all important presence of the KKK turbocharger, pushed the power developed by the overhead-camshaft four to 170bhp, which compared with a figure of 125bhp for the standard unit.

Unlike the engine of the mainstream car, this was built at Porsche's Zuffenhausen factory, rather than at Neckarsulm.

Further changes were made to the suspension whilst ventilated disc brakes, courtesy of the 911,

now featured at the front and rear. First and second gears in the strengthened gearbox were lowered.

Outwardly the 924 Turbo closely resembled the basic model although intakes were introduced just above and below the front bumper to route air to the air cooler and brakes.

A turbocharged engine gets hotter than a normally aspirated unit so a NACA duct was introduced into the bonnet so that hot air could escape from the engine compartment when the car was stationary.

Below: The Porsche 924 Turbo, identified by its bumper level air intakes for the air cooler and brakes.

At the rear of the car, a polyurethane spoiler was introduced around the window, which contributed to a marginally reduced drag coefficient.

The 924 Turbo's thin spoked alloy wheels were also new, as were their five-stud fixings.

These ministrations pushed the model's top speed to 225km/h (140mph), and the Turbo was able to reach 100km/h (62mph) in a respectable 7.8 seconds.

If the car had a weakness it was that the turbocharger had a tendency to cut in rather quickly, a shortcoming that Porsche strove to resolve for the 1981 model year. Then the original turbocharger was replaced with a smaller, more responsive unit. As a result power was increased to 177bhp and top speed to 230km/h (143mph).

But for all the model's potential, sales were relatively disappointing. The Turbo was therefore discontinued in mid-1982, after a modest four-year manufacturing life, by which time some 12,000 examples had been built.

SPECIFICATION	PORSCHE 924 TURBO
ENGINE	Turbocharged straight 4, 1984cc
HORSEPOWER	170bhp @ 5800rpm
TRANSMISSION	Manual 5-speed
CHASSIS	Unitary
SUSPENSION	Independent front and rear
BRAKES	Hydraulic disc
TOP SPEED	225km/h (140mph)
ACCELERATION	0-96km/h (60mph): 7.1 seconds

Above: The model endured for a mere four years, being discontinued in 1982 by which time Porsche was concentrating its resources on the 944. Below: The Porsche 924 Turbo's engine featured a completely new cylinder head casting although the bottom of the 2 litre four required no strengthening.

Porsche 944

THE THIRD of the new generation of front-engined Porsches, the 944, which contained elements of both the 924 and 928, appeared in 1981.

Here was a model much more in the Porsche traditions, a 217km/h (135mph) coupé with sparkling acceleration and superlative handling. Some 90,000 were built during a 10-year manufacturing life.

The coupé bodywork was related to that of the 924 although it was 50mm (2in) wider. It also featured larger wheels with flared arches and a frontal polyurethane air dam.

The four-cylinder, 2.5 litre, single-overhead-camshaft engine was, in effect, one bank of the 928's V8 unit with an enlarged 100mm bore although the 78mm stroke was retained. However, such large capacity fours have a reputation for roughness higher up the rev range.

This had been an all-too-obvious bugbear on the 924's Audi unit, so for its own engine Porsche introduced a pair of contra-rotating shafts to counter the secondary forces.

Like the 924 and 928, the 944's Audi-based five-speed gearbox was an intrinsic part of a transaxle and separated from the engine by the now familiar tubular backbone. The all-independent suspension was 924-related and uprated accordingly.

Below: The 924/928-related 944. This is a British-registered 1986 944 Lux entry-level model, by which time it had acquired 928-style wheels.

Left: The 2.5 litre, Porsche-designed, single-overhead-camshaft, four-cylinder 944 engine, which is effectively half a 928 unit.

Below: The 944S, introduced in 1986 with the 2.5 litre engine now featuring a 16-valve, twin-overhead-camshaft cylinder head.

Unlike the two other models which were only available in closed forms, there was to be a cabriolet version of the 944. But although the factory exhibited a 'study' in 1985, it did not enter production until the 1988 arrival of the S2 version, that is considered separately.

The 944 soon gained a justifiable reputation for excellent performance and handling. It acquired power steering in 1984 and a turbocharged version followed in 1985.

The 944S arrived for the 1987 season with a 16 valve, twin-overhead-camshaft cylinder head that pushed brake horsepower up from 163 to the 190 mark.

The S was positioned between the 944 proper and the Turbo and benefited from modifications that had already been applied to the US-designated 928S of 1985. This had featured an enlarged 4.9 litre engine, which shared the same 100mm bore with the 944.

The 944S was, therefore, the recipient of one of the 928S's new cylinder heads, that was also extended to the 928S-4, simultaneously announced with the four-cylinder model.

The S was capable of 228km/h (142mph) and had the virtue of not being affected as adversely by emissions equipment as the basic 944. It evolved into the 3 litre S2 .

For its part the single-cam model was at the same time enlarged to 2.7 litres. It was built in this form until production ceased in 1991.

SPECIFICATION	PORSCHE 944
ENGINE	Straight 4, 2479cc
HORSEPOWER	160bhp @ 5800rpm
TRANSMISSION	Manual 5-speed
CHASSIS	Unitary
SUSPENSION	Independent front and rear
BRAKES	Hydraulic disc
TOP SPEED	217km/h (135mph)
ACCELERATION	0-96km/h (60mph): 8.1 seconds

Porsche 956

THE SUCCESS of the 936 encouraged Porsche to produce a successor and the result was the 956, geared to the Group C regulations of 1982. This attained new competitive heights and provided the company with an unprecedented four successive victories at the Le Mans 24 hour race.

The 956 has the distinction of being Porsche's first sporting-racing monocoque. As such the traditional chassis was dispensed with and the car powered by a mid-located, twin-turbocharged, 2.6 litre flat six engine.

The body, wind-tunnel-tested at Porsche's Weissach research and development facility opened in 1972, was notable for its twin stabilizing fins joined by a large rear wing. The latter arrested progress somewhat on straights but made the 956 faster through corners.

The works team was fortunate to obtain sponsorship from the Rothmans cigarette company, a partnership that was to endure for the next six years. The principal drivers were Jacky Ickx and Derek Bell.

After a not particularly impressive debut at Silverstone in 1982, the car did not appear again until Le Mans. There the three 956s proceeded to dominate the race with Ickx once again driving the winning car and 956s also in second and third places.

Porsche had no plans to run in World Sports Car Championship events after Le Mans, but the factory could not resist entering the Spa 1000km event 10 weeks later. Not only did the 956 win there, but also at Fuji and Brands Hatch. With such a record it came as no surprise to find that Porsche once again took the Championship for Makes title.

It retained this accolade in 1983. Le Mans fell to the triumphant 956s again that year with the cars from Stuttgart totally dominating the event by taking the first eight places.

The factory did not run in the 24 hour race in 1984 but a Reinhold Joest-entered 956, driven by Klaus Ludwig and Henry Pescarolo, won.

However, the works cars were back in 1985, along with Joest's team. Not only was the privateer victorious, but the same car, 956/117, took the chequered flag for the second year in succession.

The 956's last season was 1986 but that year its 962 stablemate won at Le Mans. Meanwhile, Joest's faithful 117 provided the 956 with its last victory at Fuji, an appropriately upbeat note on which to conclude this account of one of Porsche's most successful sports racers.

Below: The 956, Porsche's very successful sports racer that won the Le Mans 24 hour race on no less than four occasions. This is a 1982 956C in Rothmans livery which featured until 1988.

SPECIFICATION	PORSCHE 956
ENGINE	Twin turbo, flat 6, 2650cc
HORSEPOWER	630bhp @ 8200rpm
TRANSMISSION	Manual 5-speed
CHASSIS	Monocoque
SUSPENSION	Independent front and rear
BRAKES	Hydraulic disc
TOP SPEED	378km/h (235mph)
ACCELERATION	N/A

Right: The 956's bodywork was made in seven pieces of Kevlar, glass-fibre and aluminium. Below right: The Heyer/Merl/Schmickentanz 956 in the 1983 Silverstone 1000km race, won by a 956.

Porsche 911 Cabriolet

SPECIFICATION	PORSCHE 911 CABRIOLET
ENGINE	Flat 6, 2994cc
HORSEPOWER	180bhp @ 5500rpm
TRANSMISSION	Manual 5-speed
CHASSIS	Unitary
SUSPENSION	Independent front and rear
BRAKES	Hydraulic disc
TOP SPEED	246km/h (153mph)
ACCELERATION	0-96km/h (60mph): 6.2 seconds

THE NEED for an open version of the 911 had been partially met by the arrival of the Targa version in 1965, although it was not until 1982 that a true convertible made an appearance.

As already recounted, the open version of the 356 was not perpetuated with the 911. Instead the Targa, with its ingenious built-in roll-over bar, replaced it as Porsche feared that impending safety legislation in America would require its obligatory fitment.

As it happened, these fears proved to be groundless but, by the time that the risk had receded and Porsche's marketing arm was speaking of the desirability of a 911 Cabriolet, Dr Ernst Fuhrmann held the reigns at Zuffenhausen.

As he regarded the 928 as the 911's true successor, he vetoed a convertible version of the latter, although one was subversively constructed in anticipation of the chief executive's eventual departure.

This came sooner than most expected because, in downgrading the 911, Fuhrmann had brought himself into conflict with Ferry Porsche, who had initiated the model and was guardian of the firm's sports car origins.

Matters came to a head in 1980 when Fuhrmann's retirement was announced and his place taken, at the beginning of 1981, by the American-born German, Peter W. Schutz, whose views were more in accord with those of the chairman.

Under his tenure the 911 once again moved centre stage and the company wasted little time in exhibiting a four-wheel-drive 911 Cabriolet at the 1981 Frankfurt Motor Show. A greatly refined version of the drive system was eventually to flower in the superlative 959 in 1987, but the open 911 was a more straightforward proposition. It joined the 3 litre line in 1982.

As it happened, the removal of the Targa's roll-over bar made remarkably little difference to the rigidity of the 911's shell, although some minor reinforcement was necessary.

The Cabriolet's interior was also remarkably similar to that of the Targa whilst the hood could be raised and lowered in a single movement. To

Left: A 1983 911 Carrera Cabriolet in Martini colours and with optional flared wheel arches and rear spoiler in the manner of the top-line Turbo.

prevent any undue buffeting, the material was backed with longitudinal aluminium reinforcement. When raised, the rear window could not only be opened by a zip fastener, but was also completely detachable.

Originally offered as a 911SC option, the Cabriolet continued as the 3.2 litre Carrera for the 1984 season and in 1987 was extended to the 911 Turbo. After its belated appearance, it has remained a popular member of the 911 line ever since.

Right: A 1989 Cabriolet. Below: A 1986 model year Sport Equipment 911. However, this version for the British market lacked front and rear spoilers.

Porsche Carrera 3.2 litres

SPECIFICATION	PORSCHE CARRERA 3.2
ENGINE	Flat 6, 3164cc
HORSEPOWER	231bhp @ 5900rpm
TRANSMISSION	Manual 5-speed
CHASSIS	Unitary
SUSPENSION	Independent front and rear
BRAKES	Hydraulic disc
TOP SPEED	245km/h (152mph)
ACCELERATION	0-96km/h (60mph): 5.5 seconds

FOR THE 1984 season Porsche considerably simplified its 911 model line with the Carrera name being universally applied to the coupé, Targa and Cabriolet which were powered by a new enlarged 3.2 litre engine. They continued to be built in these forms until 1989.

As in the case of the 911 Cabriolet, these developments followed Peter Schutz's appointment as Porsche's chief executive in 1981. As a result the following year the long-neglected 911 was allotted the largest segment of the corporate development budget.

One outcome was the arrival of the 3164cc engine which represented the first major reworking of the air-cooled flat six concept since its development 20 years before.

As it happened, the capacity of the 911 Turbo's unit had already been enlarged to 3.3 litres for 1978 and in the early 1980s the company had produced some twin-turbocharged 700bhp 3.2s for owners of the sports-racing 935. These used the Turbo crankshaft in conjunction with the cylinders of the current 3 litre.

But there was much more to the 3.2 than this. It was extensively reworked, some 80 per cent was new and it developed 231bhp which compared with its predecessor's 204. This meant that the 911 could now reach 161km/h (100mph) in 13.6 seconds and had a best ever top speed of 245km/h (152mph).

Improvements were also made to the model's brakes whilst four and fifth gear ratios were uprated.

Customers could also specify the M-491 body kit which enhanced their cars with Turbo-style flared wheel arches, an option that was available across the body range.

The 1986 cars received a new fascia panel, together with improved front seats, whilst the following year's 911's were belatedly given a hydraulic clutch, in place of the cable that had sufficed since the model's inception.

These and many other modifications meant that the car remained competitive. In 1988 the 250,000th example was built and Porsche issued the Celebration 911, with distinctive metallic diamond blue paint with silver blue soft leather seats. It was available in coupé, Targa and Cabriolet forms.

This was a car that, if Dr Fuhrmann had had his way, would have ceased production in 1984. But in that year some 14,000 were built, a near annual production record for model. Here was a car that had resolutely refused to die!

Far left: The 3.2 litre engine of a 1986 Carrera.
Left: Interior with the electrical seat adjustment control, introduced in 1984, apparent. Right: 1986 Carrera, complete with interested feathered spectator!

Porsche 962

Below: A 1982 962 at the 1994 Goodwood Festival of Speed. Entered by Porsche GB, it was the Official Centre Team car at Le Mans in 1994.

WITH THE 956 dominating the World Sports Car Championship, Porsche also recognized the importance of trans-Atlantic competition as America was its most important market for road cars. In 1984 it therefore introduced the outwardly similar 962 with its mechanicals tailored for IMSA series events.

As participants were able to specify their own engine capacities, flat sixes of 2.8, 3 and 3.2 litres were variously employed. However, only a single turbocharger was permitted and the massive KKK unit, located behind the engine, dominated the rear of the car.

These States-side competitions tended to be more vigorously challenged than those held in the European arena, but the 962 was invariably victorious and won 46 IMSA races between 1984 and 1987.

A particularly impressive succession of wins came in 1986 when Al Holbert and Derek Bell not only triumphed in the 24 hour Daytona race but also drove to victory at Le Mans with Hans Stuck joining the victorious team. As if this was not enough, in the following year the 962 repeated this achievement on both sides of the Atlantic, so winning four 24-hour events in succession.

These victories were attained with the redesignated 962C, cars that in 1985 the factory had modified for Group C competition and featured twin-turbocharged engines. Water-cooled, four-valve cylinder heads were employed.

SPECIFICATION	PORSCHE 962
ENGINE	Turbocharged flat 6, 2869cc
HORSEPOWER	650bhp @ 8200rpm
TRANSMISSION	Manual 5-speed
CHASSIS	Monocoque
SUSPENSION	Independent front and rear
BRAKES	Hydraulic disc
TOP SPEED	386km/h (240mph)
ACCELERATION	N/A

Further mechanical changes came in 1986 and 1987 when the (by now) 3 litre flat sixes became fully water cooled, so dispensing with the large and distinctive cooling fan.

By this time the competition was becoming increasingly challenging, and it was in the face of a year of testing events that in 1987 a 926C again won at Le Mans. This gave Porsche seven victories in a

Below: Porsche has now won the Le Mans 24 hour race more times than any other manufacturer. The 962 was victorious on three occasions and this car is described as a Le Mans Prototype.

Above: The Japanese-entered Team Alpha 962, driven by Tiff Needell, David Sears and Anthony Reid at Le Mans in 1990, that came third behind two Jaguar XJR-12s, despite being 28th car on the grid.

row and, in doing so, it overtook the record of Ferrari that had achieved six successive wins between 1960 and 1965. The Italian firm's record total of nine victories had also fallen to Porsche in 1986.

But this was not quite the end of the story, because a full seven years after this 1987 triumph, in 1994, a 962 won at Le Mans again with Baldi, Dalmas and Haywood sharing the driving of a road-equipped car. Under new regulations this unalloyed sports racer was permitted to run as a grand tourer and it accordingly also won its class.

This brought Porsche's Le Mans victories to a total of 11, a dominance that it shows every intention of maintaining with the make again taking the chequered flag in 1996.

55

Porsche 944 Turbo

THREE AND a half years after the 944's appearance, in 1985 a turbocharged version made a welcome arrival. It greatly improved an already well received model.

Its introduction had been foreshadowed by the factory running a turbocharged 944 at Le Mans in 1981. Compared with the normally aspirated model, the new car was more accelerative and, with a top speed of 246km/h (153mph), some 10km/h (6mph) faster.

Outwardly the Turbo resembled the mainstream car, but featured a revised frontal treatment with additional air intakes while a supplementary tray was introduced at the vehicle's rear to improve undercar airflow. Another detail refinement was the provision of a flush-fitting windscreen. All of these modifications combined to improve the car's aerodynamics.

The introduction of a KKK turbocharger to the 2.5 litre four necessitated some modifications to the engine. The most significant change required strengthening the cylinder walls and stronger forged, as opposed to cast, pistons were employed. As a result of these ministrations, the 944 Turbo's engine developed 220bhp compared with 163 for the original.

In view of the increased output, the five-speed Audi gearbox was strengthened and this also applied to the differential. Braking was also improved and the increased engine weight demanded the fitment of power-assisted steering.

Wider wheels and an uprated suspension completed the mechanical modifications.

With the arrival of the 944 Turbo, Porsche took the opportunity to introduce a new fascia, which was a considerable improvement on the old one that betrayed the model's 924 Volkswagen/Audi origins. It was also notable for the use of 928 type instruments that were simultaneously fitted to the basic model.

Not only was the 944 Turbo quick, it was also agreeably quiet, regardless of speed, and performance was on a par with that of the 3.2 litre 911 Carrera.

Below: A 944 Turbo Sport of 1988. A total of 1000 examples were produced with a 250bhp engine, based on the Turbo Cup Championship cars.

SPECIFICATION	PORSCHE 944 TURBO
ENGINE	Turbocharged straight 4, 2479cc
HORSEPOWER	220bhp @ 6000rpm
TRANSMISSION	Manual 5-speed
CHASSIS	Unitary
SUSPENSION	Independent front and rear
BRAKES	Manual disc
TOP SPEED	246km/h (153mph)
ACCELERATION	0-96km/h (60mph): 6.1 seconds

In 1986 a series of Porsche Turbo Cup races were introduced in Germany and the company produced a purpose-created Turbo Cup model which retained the standard 220bhp engine but had lowered and uprated suspension. An interior roll cage was also fitted.

With the arrival, in 1988, of the S2 version of the 944, the Turbo was fitted with a larger turbocharger, which pushed power up to 250bhp, a limited slip differential and the wheels were widened still more. Production, along with that of the 944, ceased in 1991. By then a respectable 51,000 Turbos had been built.

Left: A 1987 example, outwardly similar to the unblown car but with an extra air intake. Above: Just in case there should be any doubt . . .

Porsche 928S-4

THE 928 was nine years old in 1986 when it received a body and mechanical facelift with the arrival of the S-4 version. This in turn led to the top line GT of 1989 and, ultimately, the even faster GTS unveiled in 1991.

But whilst such refinements in the 911 generated greater demand, in the case of the 928, Porsche was attempting to shore up a model for which there was only limited public appeal.

Having said that, outwardly the S-4 benefited from new sharper features, along with further improvements to its aerodynamics. This most

notably consisted of a reprofiled nose, whilst at the rear there was a new spoiler, conveniently hinged to permit washing.

The V8 engine was enlarged from 4.7 to a bigger bored 4.9 litres and each cylinder bank now employed twin-overhead-camshaft, 16-valve cylinder heads of the type that also appeared on the 944S.

American customers had already had a preview of this engine (that developed 288bhp, compared with the 4.7's disappointing 234), in what was still called the 928S which was announced at the beginning of 1985.

The intention was to boost all important trans-Atlantic sales, and shed the 928's image of an impressively engineered but gutless performer.

By the time that this same engine appeared in Series 928S-4, it had acquired an additional 32bhp and the model was now capable of 257km/h (160mph).

Yet further fire was breathed into the V8 with the arrival of the 928 GT at the beginning of 1989 that, with a claimed top speed of 274km/h (170mph), made it the fastest production Porsche road car of its day.

Below: A 928 GTS with sharper lines introduced on the S-4 and an enlarged 5.4 litre V8 engine. This car dates from 1995 that was the last year of production.

Its engine delivered 330bhp, which was 10bhp more than the S-4, and it retailed for the same price. Other changes to the specification included modified and stiffened suspension and wider wheels.

There was yet another capacity increase, to 5.4 litres, for the 928 GTS which appeared at the 1991 Frankfurt Motor Show and replaced the S-4 and GT. Now developing a massive 360bhp, the manual and automatic options were maintained.

This was the last change of any significance for the 928 which ceased production in 1995. With its demise went the last of Porsche's front-engined grand tourers, and Dr Fuhrmann's vision of moving Porsche up-market and away from its sports car roots. From there on, the Stuttgart company would concentrate on what it did best: the family of rear- or mid-engined 911-related cars.

SPECIFICATION	PORSCHE 928S-4
ENGINE	V8, 4957cc
HORSEPOWER	320bhp @ 6000rpm
TRANSMISSION	Manual 5-speed
CHASSIS	Unitary
SUSPENSION	Independent front and rear
BRAKES	Hydraulic disc
TOP SPEED	257km/h (160mph)
ACCELERATION	0-96km/h (60mph): 6.3 seconds

Top: A 1988 928S-4, which featured combined spot, fog and indicator lamps. Above: The comfortable 928S-4 interior with electrically adjustable seats. Air conditioning was a standard fitment to this model.

Porsche 959

THE FOUR-wheel-drive 959 was Porsche's first and only supercar. After a protracted gestation, it finally appeared in 1987. Just 220 examples of this fabulous 314km/h (195mph) coupé were built.

Created under the management of Peter Schutz, the 911-related 959 was a statement that, despite an apparent switch to front-engined grand tourers, Porsche was still very much in the sports car business.

As with so many exercises, this one began with a project car. It appeared at the 1983 Frankfurt Motor Show as a Group B four-wheel-drive car and was clearly intended for such competition. As it happened, the events for which it was designed were abandoned in 1986. But what was to become the 959 was also to be offered for public sale as an exclusive and costly road car.

It was eventually priced at DM 420,000 (£140,000) and the company was inundated with orders from prospective customers. But a projected initial 1985 delivery date came and went and it was not until April 1987 that the first 959 was delivered.

The car's sophisticated four-wheel-drive system had, in the meantime, been proving its worth in the sands of Africa. In 1986 a trio of pre-production 959s entered the demanding Paris to Dakar Rally and came in first, second and sixth.

Below: This is a rare Sport version of the 959; just six examples were built and it was some 100kg (220lb) lighter than the original model. It was devoid of such creature comforts as air conditioning, electric windows and right-hand external mirror.

Above: A 959 on the move. The model was only produced in left-hand-drive form.

These cars bore a close resemblance to the 959 proper that outwardly resembled the 911. However, much of the body was made of a plastic material of a type that was more associated with the aircraft than the motor industry. It was consequently some 50 per cent lighter than its steel equivalent.

SPECIFICATION	PORSCHE 959
ENGINE	Twin turbo flat 6, 2851cc
HORSEPOWER	450bhp @ 6500rpm
TRANSMISSION	4-wheel-drive, manual 6-speed
CHASSIS	Unitary
SUSPENSION	Independent front and rear
BRAKES	Hydraulic disc, ABS
TOP SPEED	314km/h (195mph)
ACCELERATION	0-96km/h (60mph): 3.5 seconds

The rear-located, 450bhp-twin-turbocharged, flat six engine, based on the 956/962 sports-racer, came complete with water-cooled cylinder heads. Perversely, its 2851cc capacity was unique to the 959.

A six-speed gearbox was employed and, at the heart of the drive system, was what Porsche called its control clutch. This consisted of seven outer and six inner plates running in oil which were pressed together and separated by an electrohydraulic servo motor. The computer-controlled action thus diverted the required amount of torque from the rear wheels to the front ones.

Then there was electrically controlled ride height, brakes and a computer programme to cope with four types of road conditions. All of these factors combined to produce a car that was faster than practically anything else on the road, yet was still remarkable easy to drive.

Having said that, there was some relief at Porsche when the last 959 was delivered in 1988. It had been a very costly exercise and Peter Schutz, the architect of the project, had departed in 1987 . . .

Below: The 959 Sport with interior roll-over bar.

Below: The 959's 2.8 litre, twin-turbocharged, 956/962-based engine. Below right: The low key interior was similar to the 911 Turbo. Bottom: The 959's distinctive rear view *with aerodynamic wing. Right: The 911 had used a separate front bumper but this was abandoned on the 959 for aerodynamic reasons.*

62

Porsche Carrera 4

THE 25th anniversary of the 911's launch fell in 1988 and it marked a significant milestone in the model's evolution. That year, for the 1989 season, witnessed a four-wheel-drive version of the 911, designated the Carrera 4, with revised body lines. The conventionally driven version became, in 1989, the Carrera 2.

Outwardly this model, designated 964 in Porsche's design register, retained the 911's unmistakable body lines. Across-range changes were confined to its lower section with the introduction of new deeper 928-style front and rear plastic bumpers and sills.

The contours of the front bumper were also rounded and this, when taken in conjunction with a new smoother floor pan, greatly improved the model's aerodynamic qualities.

There were also changes at the rear with the introduction of a dual function rear spoiler. Initially fitting flush with the engine cover, at 77km/h (48mph) it rose automatically to apply downforce to the rear wheels.

Below: On the Carrera 4, Porsche's torsion bar suspension was replaced by coil springs. This is a 1990 car.

SPECIFICATION	PORSCHE CARRERA 4
ENGINE	Flat 6, 3600cc
HORSEPOWER	250bhp @ 6100rpm
TRANSMISSION	4-wheel-drive, manual 5-speed
CHASSIS	Unitary
SUSPENSION	Independent front and rear
BRAKES	Hydraulic disc, ABS
TOP SPEED	259km/h (161mph)
ACCELERATION	0-96km/h (60mph): 5.3 seconds

Below the surface, the four-wheel-drive system was a simplified version of that applied to the 959. An epicyclic central differential ensured that, in the permanent driving mode, 31 per cent of power would be applied to the front wheels and 69 to the rear.

Attached to it with the customary Porsche ingenuity was an overriding computer-controlled, hydraulically activated, multi-disc clutch.

It responded to information transmitted from sensors in the anti-lock brakes which made a welcome appearance on the 911.

Should too much power be applied to the rear wheels, the clutch would tighten up to balance the power with grip and so prevent the wheels from spinning to the detriment of traction.

In addition, there were changes to the air-cooled, rear-mounted engine. The bore and stroke of the flat six were increased with the result that capacity rose from 3.2 to 3.6 litres and power to 250bhp. A new twin spark ignition system also featured.

But another sacred Porsche feature, the torsion bar suspension medium that had been

Above: The Carrera 4 dispensed with conventional bumpers.
Right: The model's new chassis resulted in the introduction of a deep transmission tunnel and stubby gear lever.

synonymous with the marque since its inception, was replaced by all-round coil springs.

The sure footed attributes of four-wheel-drive, coupled with mechanical improvements, made the Carrera 4 a 259km/h (161mph) car. It remained in production in this form until mid-1994, by which time the rest of the 911 range had undergone a further and even more visually radical update.

Porsche Speedster

BECAUSE OF the growing strength of the German mark in 1980s, Porsche was having a difficult time selling its products in America. It responded in 1988 by reviving the concept of the 356 Speedster of the 1950s although, inevitably, this latterday open two-seater was 911-based.

Conceived by chief executive Peter Schutz for what he identified as 'the entertainment market', the intention was to position the Speedster at the bottom of the range and price it at below DM100,000 (£34,000). Thus dwindling sales of the four-cylinder 924 and 944 would be redressed.

The Speedster generated considerable interest when it was unveiled as a concept car at the 1987 Frankfurt Motor Show. But this was perhaps more on account of its curious plastic tonneau which covered the entire cockpit and only permitted the driver's body to project above it.

The original Speedster was a no-frills, low cost model and the idea was a little clumsily revived on this show car. The idea was that the Speedster would be driven in its normal guise during the week but, come the weekend, the windscreen would be removed, and a roll-over bar and the substantial tonneau fitted. But even at Frankfurt applying this unwieldy lid took some 20 minutes to effect.

Peter Schutz left Porsche at the end of 1987 and by the time that the Speedster appeared in the 1989 model line, the concept had changed somewhat. Happily the ugly tonneau had disappeared. The car's body was based on that of the Cabriolet and its

running gear on the 911 Carrera which meant its 231bhp 3.2 litre engine. By this time the price in Britain had risen to £56,000.

As such it was cheaper than the 911 Cabriolet with which it shared many components although it was some 70kg (154lb) lighter. Porsche claimed that

it was rather quicker and, with the 3.6 litre engine that arrived in 1989, had a marginally higher top speed of a rather blusterous 261km/h (162mph).

The reality was that this was something of a fun car aimed at trans-Atlantic customers who already owned a 928 or Carrera 4.

For despite the Speedster being available in Britain, it was really tailored for use on the American west coast, just as the original had been. This was underlined by the fact that when the

SPECIFICATION	PORSCHE SPEEDSTER
ENGINE	Flat 6, 3600cc
HORSEPOWER	250bhp @ 6100rpm
TRANSMISSION	Manual 5-speed
CHASSIS	Unitary
SUSPENSION	Independent front and rear
BRAKES	Hydraulic disc
TOP SPEED	261km/h (162mph)
ACCELERATION	0-96km/h (60mph): 5.7 seconds

familiar, low-browed but rudimentary hood was raised, the car's occupants tended to get wet!

The Speedster remained part of the Porsche model line until it was discontinued in 1989, but was briefly revived in Carrera 2-based form in 1993.

Below: A 1989 Speedster; most were sold on the American market. Right: The 3.6 litre engine. Below right: The distinctive rear deck under which the hood was stored. Otherwise it had much in common with the Cabriolet.

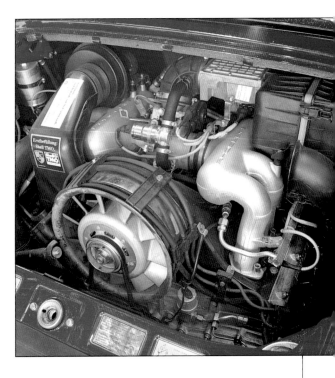

Porsche 944S2

THE 944S was given a new lease of life for the 1989 season when it was revised and improved as the S2. Hitherto the model had only been available in coupé form, but the arrival of the S2 saw the introduction of a long anticipated cabriolet version.

In its original form the S was positioned between the base model and the 944 Turbo. The S2 outwardly differed from its predecessor by inheriting the Turbo's body, but with the twin-overhead-camshaft, 16-valve four enlarged from 2.7 to 3 litres.

The engine was also lighter than its predecessor with thinner walls and water depth increased around the cylinder liners.

It developed 211bhp, of which Porsche claimed that 3bhp was contributed by the introduction of holes at the base of each pair of cylinder liners. This permitted the air trapped beneath one downcoming piston to be transferred into the low pressure space between its adjacent and rising opposite number.

Both of these improvement are of interest on a broader canvas because they were inherited from the Formula 1 V6 engine that Porsche designed for the TAG (Techniques d'Avant Garde) concern to power the McLaren racing cars that secured the world championship in the 1984-86 seasons.

In view of the extra power, the S2 used the Turbo's more robust five-speed gearbox whilst the wheels were also wider than those employed hitherto. Anti-lock brakes were standardized.

On the road the enlarged engine proved itself to be a good and wholly consistent puller, although with some body roll at lower speeds. Handling,

Below: A 1989 model year 944S2 that employed the 944 Turbo's body but was mechanically transformed by the presence of an enlarged 3 litre engine. Handling was excellent and unaffected by the extra power.

SPECIFICATION	PORSCHE 944S2
ENGINE	Straight 4, 2990cc
HORSEPOWER	211bhp @ 5800rpm
TRANSMISSION	Manual 5-speed
CHASSIS	Unitary
SUSPENSION	Independent front and rear
BRAKES	Hydraulic disc
TOP SPEED	240km/h (149mph)
ACCELERATION	0-96km/h (60mph): 6.2 seconds

Left: The long-awaited 944S2 Cabriolet. The windscreen was slightly lower than the coupé's and the hood electrically operated.

always a 944 strong point, was unaffected by the more powerful engine and the S2 remained a well balanced car.

The company claimed a top speed of 240km/h (149mph) which was 11km/h (7mph) more than its predecessor.

These attributes also applied to the open version of the S2 and the Cabriolet was fitted with an electrically operated hood. This was secured to a windscreen that was 60mm (2.4in) lower than the coupé's and stowed quite flat so as not to restrict rear visibility.

In its final manifestation in 1991, the outwardly unchanged open car was offered in turbocharged form, but this limited edition model was supplied with high levels of equipment that included sports suspension and air conditioning.

This, in turn, paved the way for what was informally known as the 944S3, but was announced for 1992 as the 968 model.

Right: The large tailgate, complete with aerodynamic spoiler, was a common feature of the 944, 924 and 928. The S2's body was essentially that of the 944 Turbo.

69

Porsche 968

THE 944 ceased production after a 10-year manufacturing life in 1991, when it was replaced by the 968. Rooted in the 944 concept, it was not the best received of Porsche models and this, combined with the economic recession, meant that it never sold in the anticipated numbers.

The 968 was, in effect, a rebodied 944 with a front end, complete with the flush-mounted headlamps, clearly related to the 928. A new tail completed the package.

The 944's 3 litre engine was also carried over, although ministrations, in particular to its inlet manifold, resulted in a 10 per cent increase in power, to 240bhp. It also received a variable valve-timing mechanism that Porsche patented as Variocam. This altered valve timing at higher revolutions and so increased engine output.

A further innovation was the introduction of a Getrag six-speed gearbox in place of the five-speed unit employed on the 944. Porsche's efficient Tiptronic four-speed automatic gearbox was an option.

Like its predecessor, the 968 was available in coupé and cabriolet forms. But whilst its roadholding was well up to the standard of its predecessor, there was some disquiet voiced by commentators who suggested that the ageing big four tended to lack refinement, particularly at lower revolutions.

Sales also proved to be sluggish at a time of recession, and for 1993 Porsche introduced the lighter 968CS, for Club Sport, model which was some 18 per cent cheaper than the coupé that continued in production.

As a weight-saving exercise, such items as electric windows and the model's minuscule rear seats were dispensed with, changes that saved some 50kg (110lb). Handling was also improved by lowering the suspension 20mm (0.8in), to the extent that *Autocar & Motor* magazine judged it to be the best-handling car of 1993.

Below: The 968's 944 origins are all too apparent.

SPECIFICATION	PORSCHE 968
ENGINE	Straight 4, 2990cc
HORSEPOWER	240bhp @ 6200rpm
TRANSMISSION	Manual 6-speed
CHASSIS	Unitary
SUSPENSION	Independent front and rear
BRAKES	Hydraulic disc, ABS
TOP SPEED	251km/h (156mph)
ACCELERATION	0-96km/h (60mph): 6.2 seconds

Above: A 1993 968 Cabriolet with its hood up. As an open car, it has a different rear section to the coupé's.
Left: The model with its hood neatly stowed away. There were two small rear seats.

That same year saw the introduction of the 968 Turbo S created for the new German GT Series racing events. Developing 305bhp, this was a limited production model, capable of 282km/h (175mph) and built on a special production line at Porsche's Weissach research centre.

But despite the 968's undoubted qualities, the model, rooted as it was in 1970s technology, only enjoyed a four-year manufacturing life and was discontinued in 1995. It was soon to be followed by its 928 stablemate.

Porsche 911 Carrera & Turbo

WHEN THE 911 was revised for the 1989 model year, outward modifications were confined to the bumpers and sills. But changes applied to the 1994 cars were far more radical. Although this new generation of cars were still identifiably Porsches, they did represent the most significant stylistic modifications in the model's history.

Interestingly the visual revisions, that drew inspiration in part from the 968 and 959 cars, were the work of Porsche stylist, Tony Hatter, an Englishman.

The most obvious difference was the arrival of flared arches to accommodate the new, wider wheels. At the front there were new contoured bumpers, the wings were accordingly flattened and the oval headlamps nestled into the bodywork to a greater degree than their predecessors.

The side and rear windows were now virtually flush, as opposed to being recessed with the bodywork, which helped the aerodynamics. In addition a small spoiler was introduced just above the rear window.

Below the surface this 911 was a beneficiary of a new chassis with weight savings being made by the adoption of all-round aluminium wishbones. These were used in conjunction with the customary MacPherson struts at the front, but there was a new multi-link layout at the rear that replaced the semi-trailing arms previously employed.

The current top-of-the-range Turbo is the most impressive version yet of this illustrious

Above: Those unmistakable Porsche lines remain intact on this 1996 member of the Carrera dynasty.

Below: Top-of-the-range Turbo which combined the virtues of a 3.6 litre, twin-turbocharged engine and the roadholding of four-wheel drive. The massive ventilated disc brakes are very efficient. This is a 1995 car.

73

SPECIFICATION	PORSCHE 911 CARRERA TURBO
ENGINE	Twin turbo, flat 6, 3600cc
HORSEPOWER	408bhp @ 5750rpm
TRANSMISSION	4-wheel-drive, manual 6-speed
CHASSIS	Unitary
SUSPENSION	Independent front and rear
BRAKES	Hydraulic disc, ABS
TOP SPEED	290km/h (180mph)
ACCELERATION	0-96km/h (60mph): 4.3 seconds

Left: The driving compartment of a 1995 Carrera Turbo.

model. Not only does it incorporate twin turbochargers, but it also possesses the additional virtues of four-wheel-drive.

This is a 290km/h (180mph) car that can reach 100km/h (62mph) in under five seconds.

The 3 .6 litre flat six engine developed no less than 408bhp and a significant feature was that it employed two KKK turbochargers. These guaranteed a significant improvement in throttle response over the single large unit previously employed with no attendant loss of performance.

The four-wheel-drive system is an improved version of that already employed on the Carrera 4

that was similarly refined for the 1995 season. It features a viscous clutch and an automatic brake differential that recognizes the slip on individual wheels, cutting drive from the spinning wheel to the one with grip.

The ABS brakes, even by Porsche standards, are extraordinarily impressive and the all-round cross-drilled and ventilated discs are activated by an electro-hydraulic booster.

In addition to its phenomenal performance, Porsche claim that the Turbo can be braked from 100km/h (62mph) to standstill in just 2.6 seconds. Need we say more?

Porsche 911 GT2

THE MOST potent offering in Porsche's 1995 range was the GT2 that was little more than a road-equipped sports racer which, claimed the company, was capable of 294km/h (183mph) . . .

With a specification geared to that year's Global Endurance GT Series races, it was so called because of its participation in the popular but less powerful GT2 class. For the record, the GT1 field embraced cars that developed in excess of 450bhp, whilst Porsche's principal GT2 rival was the McLaren F1 GTR which, in the event, proved to be all conquering.

The Porsche was based on the already potent Turbo 911 but bereft of its four-wheel-drive.

Modest refinements to the twin-turbocharged engine saw output raised from an already formidable 408 to 430bhp.

Performance was greatly enhanced by a stringent policy of weight saving. As a result the GT2 had doors and bonnet made from thin-gauge aluminium rather than steel.

Below and right: Wolf in wolf's clothing, a GT2 for the road. The bonnet and doors were aluminium rather than steel. Note the distinctive rear spoiler.

The wing extensions were plastic, chosen not so much because they were lighter, but to aid their replacement during a race.

Inside, the Turbo's customary comfortable leather-upholstered seats were replaced by slim racing bucket ones. The rear seats were dispensed with altogether. In addition, sound proofing, air bags, door handles, central locking system and even the sunroof were sacrificed.

Chassis refinement included a greatly stiffened suspension, which was 20mm (0.8in) lower than the Turbo's.

Outwardly the GT2 could be identified by its movable front spoiler and massive rear wing. The handsome and stylish five-spoked wheels, noticeably larger at the back than the front, had light alloy rims with magnesium centres.

All of these ministrations produced savings of 285kg (628lb), and the GT2 weighed in at 1215kg (2679lb).

The company claimed that it could reach 100km/h (62mph) in just 4.4 seconds, which was marginally quicker than the Turbo on account of it having shed precious pounds.

On the road the GT2 was king and could hold its own against almost all-comers, with the exception of a handful of much more expensive supercars. Having said that, this performance plus Porsche retailed for some £131,000. And there were just 50 of them!

SPECIFICATION	PORSCHE 911 GT2
ENGINE	Twin-turbo flat 6, 3600cc
HORSEPOWER	430bhp @ 5750rpm
TRANSMISSION	Manual 6-speed
CHASSIS	Unitary
SUSPENSION	Independent front and rear
BRAKES	Hydraulic disc ABS
TOP SPEED	294km/h (183mph)
ACCELERATION	0-96km/h (60mph): 3.9 seconds

Above: A GT2 being demonstrated at the 1996 Goodwood Festival. The plastic wing extensions are readily apparent.

Porsche 911 Targa

THE WELL proven Targa concept, discontinued in 1993, was impressively updated for the 1996 season with the arrival of a greatly improved version.

This maintained the concept of the original in offering the open-air motoring of a cabriolet and the security and weather protection of a coupé.

At the heart of this latter day Targa is a new roof system that incorporates an electrically controlled movable glass panel extending from the windscreen through to the rear of the 911.

At the touch of a button, two minuscule electric motors activate the glass roof which slides back below the fixed rear window leaving the roof completely open. At this point a narrow glass wind deflector comes into play to minimize noise and draught.

This roof is thermally insulated and contains a special ultra-violet filter to protect the car's occupants from glare and heat. In addition, an electrically operated roller blind helps to keep the interior temperature down to much the same level as in the coupé. Air conditioning is fitted as standard.

The large rear window, which is unique to the Targa, contributes to the sense of space that is a feature of the model. And although the Targa has a higher roof line than the coupé, the mechanism of the retractable roof does reduce head room for some rear passengers.

Below: The second generation Targa with its retractable roof panel in the closed position. It has the advantage of retaining the famous profile in a way that the Cabriolet does not. Build quality has been praised – since 1988 all 911s have benefited from new production facilities at Porsche's Stuttgart factory.

SPECIFICATION	PORSCHE 911 TARGA
ENGINE	Flat 6, 3600cc
HORSEPOWER	285bhp @ 6100 rpm
TRANSMISSION	Manual 6-speed
CHASSIS	Unitary
SUSPENSION	Independent front and rear
BRAKES	Hydraulic disc, ABS.
TOP SPEED	274km/h (170mph)
ACCELERATION	0-96km/h (60mph): 5.4 seconds

This new design has only been possible because the roll-over bar, that was such a pivotal feature of the original Targa, has been replaced by two longitudinal, slim-cant rails that run from the top of the windscreen to the base of the rear window.

The model is based on the 911 Cabriolet. Despite this and the 7mm (0.3in) thick laminated glass used for the roof, the Targa is just 30kg (66lb) heavier than the 911 coupé.

In all other respects, the model benefited from all the options available on the 1996 Porsches, and a 3.6 litre engine with a choice of a six-speed manual gearbox or Tiptronic four-cog automatic. However, the new 431mm (17in) alloy wheels were peculiar to the Targa.

Thus reinvigorated, this popular 911 model seems destined for as long a manufacturing life as its famous predecessor.

Left: The Targa's roof is open. Activated by two electric motors, it slides beneath the rear glass panel. A slim wind deflector then arises at the forward edge of the hatch. The result is plenty of fresh but not draughty air.

Porsche Boxster

AN UNASHAMED backward glance at past glories provides the impetus for Porsche's open two-seater Boxster, on sale in 1997 to provide an all important second string to the 911 line.

The model began life as a concept car exhibited at the 1993 Detroit Motor Show. The Boxster name, in contrast to the usual model number, is reminiscent of two Porsche themes: namely the boxer motor, which is the European name for a horizontally opposed engine, and the famous Speedster.

Having said that, the inspiration for the Boxster's lines is the mid-engined 550 Spyder of the 1950s, that was the sports-racing version of the 356.

With a similarly located power unit, this means that it is a true two-seater that will benefit from the handling qualities that go with the configuration.

Outwardly, the car is the work of two young Porsche designers, Grant Larson and Stefan Stark, who were respectively responsible for the exterior and the interior.

The silver-hued Boxster generated much interest at its US launch and bristled with impressive features, particularly the asymmetric headlamps, curved doors and five-spoked, competition-related wheels.

Inside there were individually tailored seats, distinctive back-lit instruments and exposed gear linkage. However, some commentators were sceptical of how many of these elements would survive into production.

Below: The mid-engined, two-seater Boxster for the 1997 season with its hood raised. Electrically activated, it takes a mere 12 seconds to open, has a lightweight magnesium frame and is a snug fit so that conversations can easily take place at high speeds.

SPECIFICATION	PORSCHE BOXSTER
ENGINE	Flat 6, 2.5 litre
HORSEPOWER	204bhp
TRANSMISSION	Manual 5-speed
CHASSIS	Unitary
BRAKES	Hydraulic disc, ABS
TOP SPEED	241km/h (150mph)
ACCELERATION	0-96km/h (60mph): 6.7sec

The finished car is, in fact, outwardly similar to the 1993 show car but some changes have been necessitated by practicalities. The original front wings, for instance, were not wide enough to accommodate a radiator apiece.

This is because the mid-located, flat six, 2.5 litre engine is water-cooled, as opposed to air-cooled – a feature that will be extended to the 911.

Right: The 1993 showcar's distinctive instrument panel.
Below: The Boxster concept car.

Likewise the original low-mounted engine air intakes were found to be inadequate and have been replaced by repositioned larger ducts. In practice, the memorable curved doors were found to impede rather than aid access and they now have more conventional contours.

The company is aiming to sell between 15,000 and 20,000 examples a year and it hopes that the allure of its name, together with the two-seater's undoubted appeal, will mean that the Boxster enjoys a long production run. With Porsche's long-term future as an independent manufacturer still in question, it needs to.

Index

Page numbers in **bold** type refer to illustrations